Praise for
GET THERE NOW

"Susanne's vulnerable and honest approach to living a life of choice and possibility will awaken your passion to pursue endless possibilities every day. *Get There Now* takes you deep into moments of self-discovery, realization, even tragedy—and guides you to embrace your imperfections and create the space required to make a shift in your life, from the miniscule to the monumental."

—Shannon Wilson, co-founder, lululemon and imagine1day, Lightyear coach, mother, philanthropist

"In her powerful debut, *Get There Now*, Susanne Conrad helps you reimagine life's obstacles and transform them into powerful stepping stones on your unique path of creating a life you love. A true modern-day energy alchemist, she shares her decades-long legacy of leadership work and unique ability to 'tune' the self-discovery process in an empowering way. Susanne's wit, warmth, and challenging questions encourage a simultaneous new discovery of self while reminding us of who we actually are. If you are ready to reset and ditch old or incorrect narratives about your life in the most profound and efficient way possible, look no further than Susanne Conrad as your guide! Her process is what you've been waiting for."

—John Brenkus, six-time Emmy Award-winning producer and host, *ESPN Sport Science*, *New York Times* bestselling author, *The Perfection Point*

"Susanne has written a book that will change people's lives. I have had the opportunity to study with Susanne for eleven years, and I can attest to the power of the approach to life she shares. You will experience breakthroughs in your relationship with yourself, your relationship with others, and your relationship with Spirit."

—**Margo Downs,** former CHRO Stitch Fix, "head of people" at lululemon, advisor, dog mom, fashion and sports aficionado

"Susanne Conrad has spent her life inspiring those around her to dream bigger and get the most out of life. Her captivating stories and the insight from each will unlock a future you didn't know you were capable of. *Get There Now* will redefine what you believe possible in business and life."

—**Braden Parker,** co-founder and CEO, Casca Designs Inc.

"Susanne's work is a breakthrough in untapping pent-up human potential, a rare gift that unlocks the unrealized energy in organizations. A gifted luminary and teacher, she has an unmatched ability to take theoretical ideas and make them practical. Her work is widely accessible, transforming philosophy into lived actions. [This is] a book not to be missed."

—**Mo Jessa,** president, Earls Kitchen + Bar

"In her book, *Get There Now*, Susanne uses personal anecdotes and stories punctuated with meaningful questions to illustrate the genesis of her approach to leadership and life. As I read, I allowed myself (i.e., made the choice) to feel the emotions that resonated within her stories and reflect on their honesty and integrity. One moment I was swept up in the playfulness of the story, and the next moment, near tears as I reflected on and contrasted her life with my own experiences. Thanks to Susanne, I'm making daily choices to 'Get There Now.'"

—**Scott Elliott,** executive director, Dr. Peter AIDS Foundation

Transform Yourself and the World Through
Laughter, Listening, and the Power of Choice

GET THERE NOW

SUSANNE CONRAD

RIVER GROVE
BOOKS

Published by River Grove Books
Austin, TX
www.rivergrovebooks.com

Distributed by River Grove Books

Design and composition by Greenleaf Book Group
Cover design by Greenleaf Book Group
Cover Image: Pin free icon from Flaticon.com

Publisher's Cataloging-in-Publication data is available.

Trade Paperback ISBN: 978-1-63299-398-4

Hardcover ISBN: 978-1-63299-399-1

eBook ISBN: 978-1-63299-400-4

First Edition

To Brett (No-Middle-Name) Conrad for choosing Love
and
To Dorothy Wood Espiau for loving Choice

Contents

Preface

The Line of Choice

Mt. Rainer, Washington
Wellspring Spa
January 19, 2019
7:07 a.m.

Encouraged by my dear friend to return to Mt. Rainer to gather the "seeds" of this book, I wake up the first morning intent on making a fire to warm the small cabin and settling in with a cup of tea to begin writing. With clothes and socks on—not my contact lenses yet—I step out onto the front porch to gather dry wood from under the cabin's eave, closing the door behind me.

I hear a *click* as the door locks. *Oops.*

Barely able to see in the predawn darkness, I am stuck with no shoes, no coat, and no key back to the warmth awaiting inside. It is raining. I listen and hear the sound of someone chopping wood. I walk through the puddles of rock and mud down the road, listening for the chop and allowing it to come closer, imagining that surely someone up this early has their life together . . . and possibly a key.

I emerge at the edge of the parking lot, where I spot a man breathing heavily and hefting an axe high over his head. The *rrrrgh* of wood splitting open echoes, and a piece falls in slow motion onto the pile beside it.

I am in great hope that he has a master key, which all men who split wood in the wee hours have in my "Hope as Strategy" world. I walk gingerly over the wet gravel and puddles with tiny wood shavings floating in them, wondering, *If I lost those twenty-two pounds twenty years ago, would the stones still feel so hard? Do skinny women float over sharp things?* Perhaps my earthy heft will preserve me, however, if I must be made to endure the cold and damp. My mind wanders in a muddle, knowing it has made a mistake literally first thing in the morning, and, approaching the stranger, I struggle to gather language. I am within twelve feet now.

"Hi! Good morning!" I wave, so as not to startle the man and give him the benefit of the sound of my voice and sight of my extended arms and open palms, which provide balance with each tender step of progress. He looks up at me, tilting his head, curious. Beads of sweat and rain trickle down his forehead.

Trusting humor to help us both in the semidarkness, I establish eye contact and yell, "I was out for an early morning stroll without my contacts, socks and shoes, and coat . . ." I giggle and direct my hands to show him my bare feet perched on a large single river stone. He releases his grip on the axe, the blade stuck firmly in the stump, and his eyes widen.

"Nah, just kidding!" I laugh again, and he shares a broad, close-lipped smile.

"Truth be told, I totally accidentally locked myself out of my cabin!" Feeling an automatic need not to sound like a city dork, I add, "I stepped onto the porch to get wood to stoke last night's fire, and the door locked behind me. I am *really* hoping you have a key to let me back in."

With the deep realism of a woodsman, he says, "Hmmm. I could call Dianne the cleaning lady and see if she's got some keys. Maybe she's up . . . she don't live too far away."

My heart sinks in my chest as I blot out pictures of spending the next hour or so huddled in his truck—the idea of never warming up ever again in my life crossing my mind. "Hold the course steady, Suzy, and *be here*," I radio back from my higher self.

He dials Dianne on speaker from his cell phone. *Ring, ring, ring, ring, ring.*

"This is Dianne. Leave a message after the beep," echoes her gruff, rural Washington, cleaning-lady voice recording. *Oh dear God, she's not there.*

"Hey, Dianne, I got a lady here that's locked outta her cabin . . ."

I hear a click. *Is it possible that people still have landlines?*

"Chuck?" a woman's voice asks.

My spine straightens and my ribs rise with the breath of possibility.

Why would anyone send a guy to chop wood for their rustic spa without giving him a master key? Of course, in my universe they would . . . and oh, no, I can't feel my feet anymore.

"Okay, Chuck, here's what you need to do . . ." Her voice is gravelly, direct, and reassuring. The voice of Houston for the *Apollo* 13 astronauts. "Go to the welcome kiosk where she got her keys last night. There are little lockboxes there. The code for her cabin is one . . . three—"

Chuck is scrambling for something to write on, while I commit the numbers indelibly to memory like my address as a five-year-old child: Route Two, Box 122A, Burton, Washington.

Dianne continues, "Five . . . seven . . . two."

1-3-5-7-2. 1-3-5-7-2. 1-3-5-7-2. The numbers enter deeply on all levels of my numbing brain: my Wellspring Spa name, rank, and serial number. Chuck and I walk the rocky distance that might have been excruciating, yet as fortune and biology would have it, my feet are on fire from the freezing rain, and the tingling heat blocks the rockiness. We locate the lockbox for my cabin. It's dark, and the kiosk is without lights, save the cool white-blue of LED Christmas twinkles remaining in mid-January.

His ungloved hands now feel the cold, and perhaps needing reading glasses himself, he guesses as to which of the tiny buttons to press. One try, two tries, three tries; no opening. I bend very, very close to use my natural nearsightedness to my advantage, seeing the sequence of buttons, and gestalt the pattern of the all-powerful 1-3-5-7-2. Better than that, I see a small switch that reads "clear." I privately postulate that Chuck's attempts have failed less from a faulty sequence and more likely from the lack of "clearing" the box after each attempted code entry.

I sense Chuck is now entering save-the-damsel-in-distress mode (well, save the fifty-to-sixty-something-year-old woman with wet socks, uncombed hair, and unbrushed teeth). I am wanting to be saved, and I am about to be saved, but the geometry is such that I now have the knowledge to save myself. Yet kindness guides me to grant him his full and deserving hero-ship.

Realizing I must lovingly and gently disengage him from his task of fruitlessly punching numbers in the dark, I say, "Chuck, I can see the little numbers and a 'clear' button. Let me see if we can reset it." Standing close, his right temple to my left, the box opens. The key drops into my hand.

We glance at each other and grin.

"Thank you so much!" I say. "This is great! Okay, I'll let myself back in and put the key back in the box."

He smiles and hands me the card he has written the code on.

Micro-drama resolved, and after sending a more-than-midlife maiden on her way, Chuck asks, "How long have you been out here?"

"Oh, not too long," I reply.

"How'd you find me in the dark?"

"I listened. Heard you chopping."

"I wondered if I was waking folks."

"Thank God you were up!" My love for his morning presence spreads like butter on a hot fresh muffin.

Chuck nods, wishes me well, and returns to his truck and to the wood awaiting his axe.

Sunlight is beginning to reach through the rain as I arrive at my cabin, unlock the door, and bring in the wood I went out to get in the first place.

I don't realize until later that I've already been given the seeds of this book.

I'd locked myself out of my own life, and to return, I had to listen, go on a journey, ask for help, get correct information, use the clearing switch, enter the code, and get the key.

$$\cdots$$

My father never forgot a face or a name. My mother has a photographic memory and is a speed-reader to this day. I am neither of those things, though surely in my career both would have been immeasurably helpful. The gift I have is I can sense in the moment the issue a person is moving through at the time I meet them, and then later recall the resonance of that event. I have worked with thousands of people, some in person at conferences, over the phone, over web video, and while names, titles, and other data wash over me, when I meet them again, I am able to sense the "delta"—the shift they have made over time.

Often the shift happens in a nanosecond, while we are in each other's physical or electronic presence. It is as if my very being is a library of records, pictures of witnessing insight, of music, of harmonies, and if people are willing, I can become a tuning fork for them. I become a reminder to them of something within that they cherished and have forgotten and now is returned. Perhaps all people have this gift. If they do, they don't seem to let on much!

There was no path of "vibe-helper" that I could see as a young person. I remember taking a career-guidance test in high school. I scored high on becoming a veterinarian or physical therapist or bartender. I was told I was intelligent, yet too sensitive for many careers such as a surgeon or executive. I studied many things in an "applied" sort of way and eventually graduated in over six years with a BA in Communications and several accidental minors: one in International Public Health, one in Early Stage Motherhood, and a third in Withstanding Marital Abuse and Chronic Over-Giving. All in all, the lessons of my conceptual higher education were deafened by the roar of my actual life.

As I traversed my own bumpy terrain of self-discovery, realizations, and tragedies, I began to share what I was seeing, first to myself in my own journals, and later to friends and mentors. I began exercising the muscle of bringing this vibrational awareness to language—allowing the innate intelligence of my body to speak. For me, the body's language is sensation and the soul's language is vibration. Much of the curriculum that I have licensed to companies, and now teach to Lightyear coaches worldwide, works with helping people remember their ability to use the sensations of their body to deepen their trust in themselves, their inner knowing, and their intuition.

This kind of work takes practice, though, and works best in a community context or setting. I have come to see that we *all* have the gift to become tuning forks for one another. I have also discovered that what was missing from my high school career guidance test in 1978 was "Become a Lightyear Certified Coach."

Over the past few years, whether I've been working in a start-up, an established non-profit, a yoga studio, or a large corporation, I've been asked with earnest and eager eyes, "Do you have a book?" I always reply with warmth, yet knowing I am delivering disappointment, "No, not yet." Never have I been asked, "Do you have a social learning platform that supports people in cultivating the best in themselves by creating futures that would have never existed? A place where all the people that have ever done Lightyear programs can gather on live video calls at any time to connect?" Never have I been asked that, so I'm finally giving the people what they have been asking for: a book. I give them what they have been asking for so they can understand—through the stories from my life—what they do not yet know to ask for that is already theirs: choice.

This compilation of stories gives color and heart to challenging transits when I was either able, or not able, to shift myself out of a degrading orbit. I am writing to you to give myself the room and the space to be imperfect, and in doing so, to provide you with the opportunity to shift out of a downward spiral as well.

In this book, I turn moments of my life inside out in order to provide a map for you to do the same. Every time we take the thread of forgiveness and stitch up a hole in our own pockets where our soul slips away, we make this more possible for others who watch us do it. Every time we take the balm of self-love to calm the angry skin of an old wound, we heal a person in the future who will not need to be hurt by our unhealed pain. This enables us to look at leading our lives with new eyes. My teacher Dorothy Wood Espiau once said, "People do not change—they make new choices."

"Get There Now" is a process that allows you to leap into a new future, regardless of where you are right now. Most people live the life they are going to live anyway—you could call it a default future. In the environmental law background I have, I have learned that this is called the "No-Action" alternative. It's where you keep doing what you are already doing. Even though we are taking actions, if they are not *new* actions, we will get the same result—the same future that we were going to have anyway. To create a designed future, one must recognize that new decisions and choices are required. Our brains are magnificent and will reveal their majesty when prompted with new questions. Much of my work involves helping people ask better questions.

I am writing this book to restore choice. The choice to discover, to love, to understand, to forgive, to liberate, to embrace our mess. *And* to not stop there; to actually clean it up! I have great faith that this is the key to world peace, and I offer it, for it is what I have to give.

I want to help individuals enter a place of choice in order that they gain the skills and strength to invert the spiral of brutality that they wage against themselves. There is nothing "civil" about the civil war that rages within us, yet each of us has the power to emancipate ourselves.

We are duped into thinking we already have choice! In a world where we need experts to help us clear our overconsumption of soul-dulling stuff—people like home organizers and personal assistants—it looks like we have lots of choices, so many in fact that perhaps we don't really have any.

Imagine that as we come to this wonderful Earth, we are given a full Crayola 64-pack of colors, which represent the fresh possibility of human life and our range of expression. As we are impacted, and "learn" who we are "supposed to be" and what we are "meant to do" inside the social norms of any era, the colors are broken and not available to us. If we know we can have rose peach and fern green and midnight blue, then we can recover those colors; yet if in the distress and mundanity of living we forget that the range is there for us, we do not know how to call them back or that they even ever existed.

We lose self-expression and choice with every untested belief we make real until we have only the choice between, say, green or gray. Some choice that is! Forgetting the other sixty-four colors over time becomes a standard way of life and we learn how to "make it work."

I want you to have the choice to create many futures, many innovative companies, many thriving communities—not just the green ones or gray ones that will happen anyway and are a replication of a wounded past. I write this book to share my soul, mind, will, and emotions, and express my community-based social learning platform, Lightyear, from the inside out. May we both share our sense of humor during the heavy lifting of transformation and keep our light shining! Oh, and yes . . . *Get There Now* is also a business book. A business book from the future.

1

Bring Yourself

Santa Monica, California
March 2011

"**M**om." Surya's voice is somber, thick. Not a Saturday morning hello phone call. "Mom," he says again before I can even say, "Hi, sweetheart."

"Mom, you need to call Uncle Chip right now," my eldest son continues. "The Bethesda lululemon store was broken into last night and two girls were attacked. One is in the hospital and the other one is dead." Chip is my brother-in-law and the founder of lululemon.

I signal to my youngest son, CJ, to wait to push the elevator button on the tenth floor of his orthodontist's building as I lean my hips into a high side table across from its sliding doors. I move over to the window and gaze down at the other Saturday morning braces-tightening families returning to their cars to resume their perfectly normal mornings.

CJ's fifteen-year-old eyes query mine to discover the source of our delay in leaving as he watches me listen, phone pressed to my skull, and casually checks the stability of the table—giving it a diagnostic wiggle with his left hand.

I begin to run "codes" on myself, within my mind, to restore love, forgiveness, and choice. My body-mind connection stabilizes while listening to the facts that Surya has gathered. I had learned these codes—the Positive Points—fifteen years ago from the woman who became my teacher the moment I met her work.

Our bodies hold the remembrance of accidents, shock, trauma, grief, loss, frustration, and more with the same measure—and perhaps more—that they hold the remembrance of wonder, discernment, and growth. Our bodies are living books, recording all things said and unsaid, seen and unseen. We can hold memories of stress for many years and they can act as a magnet to attract more stress, destroying our quality of life until they are cleared. How can they be cleared, you ask? That brings me back to the technique I have practiced daily since 1996: Positive Points. These are very simple energy movements for clearing the emotional stresses that keep your body traumatized. They work rapidly to place love, forgiveness, and choice back into our memory field. These things are what get deleted when we have past or present trauma. Positive Points are simple movements done with the right hand circling clockwise over points on the outside of your left calf while stating the codes for Love "2-3," Forgiveness "5-3," and Choice "6-5." Positive Points aren't like anything else you know or have experienced, yet anyone can do them, and you will know they work by how you feel.

I return to my conversation with Surya, the recently-passed-the-bar lawyer. He keeps it short. He is ever ready to provide the needed briefing, knowing I took a media fast decades ago. His succinctness and the depth of his voice are grounding.

"Okay," I say, getting my feet under me and my head centered. "Let me listen up first and then take action. Thank you, and hug Mandy." Listening up means to get calm, centered, and receive guidance from above, instead of solely reacting to the surrounding circumstances and pressures.

Mandy, my daughter-in-law, is an Educator at the Georgetown lululemon store, which means she has gone through the leadership training programs that I have helped design. Educators are not salespeople. They are powerful, intelligent people given development and self-leadership tools that allow them to lead fuller lives by creating a ten-year vision and corresponding set of health, personal, and career goals. The idea is that then they can support lululemon Guests (most companies call them customers) in creating educated and empowered choices about the clothing and health activities in their community. Depending on traffic, the Bethesda store is only 5.9 miles from Georgetown as the crow flies, and Mandy knows most all of the people in that region of lululemon, as do I.

"I'll keep you in the loop, Surya. I love you." I pause and breathe. *One is dead.*

Having a son that is twenty-one years younger than you is not like having a son that is thirty-six years younger than you. That may seem like a non sequitur, and you may be eager to learn what happens next in this story, yet what happens next is not the stuff of a murder mystery novel. What happens next is what happens next in the life of a woman entrepreneur with four kids and an eighty-something mother and a husband and a dog.

I stand outside the elevator on the tenth floor of CJ's orthodontics office, my mind muscling through the scene Surya has just described. I run different codes on myself for panic, shock, and trauma. These, along with the Positive Points codes, immediately recircuit the electrical system of my body. I can sense the hum of my entire being as it recenters, while also sensing the world of lululemon as I knew it, and my place within that world, breaking apart.

"Mom." CJ's speech is slurred by the new length of rubber bands running from canines to molars. "Mooooom." A slight grip is in his jaw, either from the tightening or from having a mother that works on weekends, answers calls at all times and places, yet sometimes still needs three "Mom"s from him to get a response. "Mooooom. Can we stop by Allan's Aquarium on the way home and get mice for Ziggy and Sunstone?"

If you have never seen a snake eat a mouse, don't worry. You can see an illustrated, less stressful visual version in the classic book *The Little Prince*. What you need to know about a snake is that it swallows its prey whole. The process takes time and leaves the snake vulnerable, as it has a new shape, cannot move as fast, and must digest the food over many weeks. Say what you will about snakes—your opinions, fears, likes, and dislikes; their association with evil and poison—they indeed represent transformation in most all wisdom traditions of the world. Let's just say they have street cred. Once on a hike in Temescal Canyon with my good friend, Dr. V., her son, Michael, and CJ, we found a complete snakeskin and could even see where she used the crack in the rocks to get leverage to push through and leave her skin and her past in the crack in the rock.

Aside from their commitment to continual, lifelong growth, their shedding of skin to allow this growth, and their primordial patience, the attribute I've learned from most without even wanting to (because the first snake I allowed CJ to keep was a green grass snake—mostly because it only ate crickets, and I was deeply trying to avoid the mice-eating species) is the ability to swallow something whole. The sheer deliberate commitment of swallowing something whole has become a metaphor for being with what *is* versus what I wish something or someone *was*; of not attempting to pick out the parts of a person or situation that I dislike or have a reaction to.

> *Swallowing whole is an act of unconditional love.*
> *Learning to take in a person as their whole self—the*
> *shadow, the light, the joy, the hurt, the entire situation.*

The opportunity *and* the tragedy come in parallel, and the gift is the acceptance of one's own self.

Snakes take time to digest. The utter vulnerability and dedication of the snake species that I've sought to avoid have become peculiar teachers and companions, escaping and lounging on the top of computers for warmth . . . testing me.

I am listening for my next step, and before I can even answer CJ, my phone rings again. It is Margo Wheeler, the Head of People Development at lululemon; my client, my friend, my partner, my student, and sometimes my teacher. These are the multidimensional roles I have learned to honor and curate. These roles spin and intersect into a gyrating sphere other people point to inside businesses and describe as trust.

CJ looks down at me with his "really?" eyes, as he already towers over me at fifteen, awaiting a response in an all-too-familiar situation of advocating for snake rights while his mom is doing whatever it is that she actually does—which to him seems like a lot of talking on the phone.

"*Yes*, we can go to Allan's," I reply to CJ, "and I am going to answer this because the first call was Surya, and he told me there was a break-in attack at the Bethesda lululemon store and one girl's in the hospital and the other one has died."

CJ's jaw and water polo shoulders release as it becomes clear to him that responding to a criminal act trumps buying crickets, worms, and mice. Plus he got his "yes" from me and he knows my word is good.

My forefinger slides across the screen of my iPhone, over the "yes" to receive the call from Margo, knowing full well what it is likely about and the importance of steadying myself. I clear my assumptions to hear what she actually needs to say, ground through the ten floors to touch the Earth herself below, and hold space in front of my heart like an empty yet sturdy basket, ready to work.

"Hey, Margo." I inhale.

"Hey, Sus." She pauses. "Do you know?

"Yes . . . some. Surya called, and you know, Mandy works the Georgetown store." My breath is slow and deliberate. "Tell me. I am here." I frame our conversation quickly so she knows I will not be shocked, and she can lean on me if needed. The beautiful yet unfunctional and fragile side table reminds me that this is no time for shallow decoration or pretense.

Surya's briefing, combined with the Positive Points, gives me the grounding to hold Margo steady and listen as she shares what she knows of the situation in Bethesda; the unknowns outweighing the knowns. She is getting on a plane tonight for Washington, D.C. We set up a call for later in the afternoon to prepare her before leaving.

There, on the tenth floor outside the ortho, a new course for my life is set by an old choice. "I bring my whole self to work" is an early declaration I created over two decades earlier as a thirty-year-old single mother pioneering communication and leadership inside a nuclear weapons trigger factory. It was the summer of 1990, mere months after the fall of the Berlin Wall, and walls in my mind were falling too. In those days, we all worked in temporary cubicles, wore pagers, drank too much bad coffee, and ate our body weight in donuts of dubious origin.

I lived in Boulder, Colorado, a community north of the Rocky Flats Nuclear Weapons Facility where I worked. For many of my professional colleagues, Boulder was considered the epitome of hippiedom, the nesting grounds for environmental activists and the curious home of the brainchild of Chögyam Trungpa and Allen Ginsberg—the Naropa University. Tibetan monks and peaceful protesters often circled the "Bomb Plant," as Rocky Flats was called, and these people were always sourced from Boulder, or so I was told. My boys attended the local Waldorf School, I was experimenting with vegetarianism, attempting to outrun my first husband, learning how to stretch dollars beyond their measure through outlet sales of outdoor clothing, and pushing my Volvo to its design limit. And . . . contemplating experiments of my own making.

One morning, I woke up with an insight and a hypothesis. What if when I sidled up to the coffee pot and assortment of donuts at the central watering hole next to our shared administrative assistant—a human with a name, which was Lynn—and when someone, anyone, asked me, "How are you?" I would actually tell them? I would test what happened if Susanne brought her whole self to work instead of leaving my passion, eccentricity, pain, and intuition at home.

Enter Dan.

A scientific colleague, native Coloradan, dad, engineer, and level-five redhead, Dan sauntered—as young athletic men seeking calories do—to the counter, poured our best-in-the-morning coffee into his "Number One Dad" mug, and innocently asked, "Hey, Susanne, how are you?"

Fish *on*! I had a live subject for my experiment, and I held my commitment to discovery higher than my fear of being scorned.

"Well, Dan, I'm a bit spent from dealing with my boys. Chandra has some learning issues that I don't know how to solve, and Surya would rather be in a normal public school, but I want to nurture his spiritual and emotional self before he has to deal with the world head-on, and my ex-husband is hanging around and I don't feel safe because he's so volatile, and I'm also concerned about the lack of true leadership here at the plant and how we're going to verify some of the softer data coming in. So are you gonna eat that chocolate donut?"

Dan looked at me and took my paragraph in whole, his crazy red hair nodding as he nabbed the chocolate old-fashioned. "Yeah, I get it. We need to rethink the data plan and how to get attention inside the system."

From that moment on, I decided to practice telling people how I really am, trusting that the reward would be greater than the risk of being judged. I will be judged either way, so might as well make a difference and move the world forward.

In this moment, all of these years later, "Bring your whole self to work" again rings true for me. I have learned and experienced so much in the previous twenty-one years, and what it means now to bring my whole self feels like an even greater risk than it did in 1990, as I have shed and grown a thousand times or more. It is as if the "s" in self becomes capitalized after hearing Surya's message. I have come this far in my fabulous and exciting career with one hand tied behind my back, and I am the one who has tied it.

"They're not ready." "I am too much." "They won't understand." "I'll lose everything I have built if I share what I know." "I'll be dismissed as an overly sensitive woman." "I will be called la-la, flaky, and non-scientific." These are the voices of the binding rope that has always had me measure my words as a consultant, be business-like, be just different enough to limbo under the wire of conformity while disguising my fifteen years of study with the unique and uncompromised Dorothy Espiau. Even my beloved husband, Brett, barely tolerates that I've spent so much energy throughout our marriage traveling four to five times per year to be in person with Dorothy, watching how she uses her "Language of Possibility" to help people restore choice in their lives—choice that has been buried by the violation and abuse of free will.

As a new kind of self-love unties my hand, I push the button for the elevator and feel my body step up and into this new self—without a three-week survey from my analytical mind.

"You ready *now*, Mom?" CJ asks with the *harrumph* on the "now." Nothing like a teenager to keep the natural in the supernatural; his large frame and practical purpose transport me back to the now.

"Yes, I'm ready." I smile at his unedited self-expression.

We step into the elevator. Facing the doors as they close, a transformation begins from the inside out, seeded by a choice; swallowing whole the enormity, the vulnerability, and the growth that will ensue. With the sense of falling, and the elevator dropping below ground zero, we exit at Level P3 and head out of the dark garage into the light of our Saturday morning. Off to Allan's Aquarium.

Over the next few weeks, I bring my full self to work as I run large teleconference calls, region by region, allowing time and space for the young lululemon employees to express themselves and understand what the attack from a fellow team member meant to them, their store, and the staff. On each call, I use the Lightyear principle "The Body Is Innately Intelligent," and share that

the safest place is in our bodies, present and responsive.

How we speak about what really matters is not done by planning it out, through rehearsal, or internal recitation, or editing. It comes from naming what is unnamed; freeing it from the clutter of meaning that holds discovery in check.

The question is always more important than the answer.

What can bringing *your* full self to work, to family, to creativity, to community, look like? What future lies in these questions? How can we face the dark in others, our situations, and ourselves without losing our light?

Let's find the answers.

2

Uncreate Beliefs

Seattle, Washington
1960

All families have stories, and this is one that was told to me about me.

The doctor explains to my mother that it will be difficult for her to have more children. My sister, Dory, was born breech, and the doctor had to break my mother's tailbone to get Dory out. There was a pregnancy between us—a little girl who reached four months inside my mother and then left this world—giving my mother only memories of a whole human being slipping out of her while laboring on the toilet.

As an adult, I have not myself experienced a miscarriage, yet in my career, I have worked with many young mothers and couples who have. Indeed, this even became a type of sub-practice inside my role at lululemon. I now have great understanding that these parents become parents and mourners of lost children, seemingly all at once and without knowledge, preparation, or a community to hold them. These parents must bear the dismissive "Oh, everybody has miscarriages" or "One in four pregnancies ends in a miscarriage" or the horrific "It really is good for the uterus to have a nice flushing out." Perhaps the hardest to hear: "It's a fetus, not a baby yet." With hormones swinging and dreams sinking, no one knows what to say. Young fathers must grieve, lacking the ability to save their child or comfort their lover or still their own broken hearts.

In 1960, I am born into this energy field, and I hold great gratitude for my unmet older sister for giving me, through the spoken and unspoken stories of her arrival, the transferred sensitivity to support the grieving parents that will one day come into my life in my forties and fifties for support.

When my mother becomes pregnant with me, it is proclaimed a medical miracle. Now living in Bellevue, Washington, with my father at a new job at the Trane company, my parents and Dory have settled into a new life and suburban home. Here is how the story goes: My mom is pregnant, and the due date arrives and no action. They wait. They monitor. They put her on a Pitocin drip, a powerful hormone used to induce labor. Nothing happens. It is soon a month past the due date. Dr. Leversee puts her on a Pitocin flood and still no labor. My dad is admitted into the same hospital for gallstones. While he's there, the doctors have my dad sign the legal document on my mother's behalf to go ahead with an emergency C-section. He also checks the "save the mother" box in the event a choice must be made between mother and child.

I am born via C-section at 9:44 p.m. on July 17, 1960, at Seattle General Hospital, unconscious from drugs and exhaustion, at 11 pounds and 9 ounces. I am rushed to an incubator, which I barely fit in. Alongside the premature babies receiving care in the nursery, the medical residents begin calling me the "college graduate." The specialists tell my parents that, due to the sustained oxygen deprivation from the extended labor, it is likely I will have significant brain damage and not develop normally. Mom with me, and Dad without his gallstones, are all discharged days later from the hospital with instructions for me to be "observed."

Mom is also told of the "inverted bell curve," meaning that statistically few children like me develop per the Dr. Spock textbooks. Many have brain damage and are at the beginning of the curve, few are average, and many have exceedingly great intelligence. My IQ has never been tested, yet I grew up in the faith and shade of the upper end of the bell curve like a vast and sturdy tree comforting my mother into the picture that I have higher odds to become exceptional. If life were a classroom with an inverted bell curve, then lots of us would have "A"s, a few of us would have "C"s, and many of us would have "F"s. Mom hangs her hopes on the edge of the curve and sees me as an "A."

On every birthday occasion, the birthday child gets to pick whatever they want for dinner. Since mine falls in the summer, I never get to take cupcakes to school, and for that, I am still in recovery, yet choosing dinner—especially one my Gramma Larson made—is a wonderful thing. I always choose homemade fried rice and hamburgers. Living on Vashon Island in the 1960s, there is only a bar called the "Alibi," which makes pies from time to time, and a Dairy Queen. That is it for restaurant choices. Suffice it to say, for more adventurous dining, one needs to travel off island.

My parents love Chinese food and often take us to Chinatown in Seattle to eat at the Hong Kong restaurant. For a kid like me, who has become a "fussy" eater, seeing things come out of the kitchen such as the unidentifiable, macerated ingredients of egg foo young or batter-fried sweet and sour shrimp with pineapple or piles of noodles with dubious sauces of unknown origin means much of it is a pass for me. When asked what I want to order, I politely ask, "May I have a hamburger?" Going forward, the Brazier burger becomes my staple, and I ask for the known. The known is presented to me, but with a side of fried rice instead of French fries, and the combination has stuck with me. For each step, for each burger that is in the realm of comfort, there is a "side" of risk.

Palos Park, Illinois

July 1969

Bacon fried crisp in its own fat drains on paper towels while my grandmother whisks a couple of eggs in a large skillet, adding the finely chopped onion, then the white rice. Her spatula turns the mixture, integrating soy sauce and crumbled bacon. A mountain of birthday homemade fried rice: a mystery broken down into components and laid out before me in a miracle of Midwestern smells.

The barbecue finishes the burgers as Gramma somehow vaporizes from the kitchen to the back porch—a superpower of being in two places simultaneously. She returns with a plate of toasted buns and grilled burgers. We gather at the table set outside in the Illinois summer humidity with vinyl place mats and unlit citronella candles to keep the mosquitos at bay during the lengthened twilight of summer evenings. The air is heavy with the dense humidity of pre-thunder, summer storm clouds.

"On the day you were born, your father was in the hospital with gallstones." My mother's eyes flash with the excitement and trauma of the past. "He was giving birth too!"

My dad is not here to nod knowingly. He is on a business trip and my birthday has fallen on a Thursday, so we'll have to celebrate in some way on his return. Yet he does not need to be at the table, for the story has such weight and character of repetition that I know his role is to nod and allow my mother to tell the tale.

"Your father had to sign a paper saying 'save the mother.'" Turning nine, I likely have heard the story at least eight times, yet this evening, I slump in my folding lawn chair, feeling an immense heaviness imagining that my father chose my mother over me. But the wafting of delicious fried rice and sizzling burgers causes me to shift gears—my small intestines clench and my hands withdraw from the table.

"Then Dr. Leversee performed an emergency C-section, the vertical kind, cutting me from the navel all the way down to get you out." My mother nods to me. The sound of her "t" at the end of "out" is sharp like the knife, as her voice tightens. "They cut against the grain of the muscles in the abdominal wall." I marvel at how my mother shares with both deep emotion and clinical anatomy. She's shown me her scar and I've seen it in the goings and comings of dressing and bathing suit changes—long and dark with soft curves of flesh coming from the center.

"Your mother was a hosiery model, you know," my grandmother chimes in, perhaps to change the direction of the conversation, or to reinforce my mother's beauty, or to indirectly express her own fearful memory of almost losing her only daughter. My mother's brother is currently living in St. Louis with brain cancer. Gramma goes there often to help his wife, my aunt, take care of him. They have two small children, my only cousins. We're driving to their home tomorrow for a visit and to see the moon landing on live television.

I know that, on one level, my parents are happy I made it to planet Earth. Yet, without a doubt, I feel I mortally wounded my mother with my very existence and brought my father to the edge of his life as well. As a nine-year-old, I have not yet developed a way to bring these thoughts and sensations to language and, if I attempt to, I risk being folded into another family story/truth: "Oh, you know Suzy. She is so sensitive." I've taken this to mean weak and unable.

These are some of the memories told to me about me. Though I do not have a recollection of my birth directly, I do have a memory of the telling of the family memories, layered with nuance and re-creation of myself. This process happens to us all, yet especially to children, whose brains are young, growing and transforming at a rapid rate.

My first actual memory is a memory from the island. I am holding my father's left hand with my right, squinting up into his face and his horn-rimmed glasses, seeing the smile of an engineer at work. The sky is blue and the sun bright, unusual for the Northwest—no wonder this is a standout memory! In my left hand, I hold the handle of a plastic pail a third my size filled with nails. I high-step my toddler legs over 2 x 4s and the large rocks that are fill-in for the bulkhead we are building to protect our property from the Puget Sound, and arrive at the front concrete pad, the beginnings of our new home. We are building our A-frame home, where I will live for the next thirteen years. I feel the happy sense of place, belonging, and purpose.

Like anything sharp, nails can be used to build or to harm. Any good Catholic will tell you they like to focus on the "he was nailed to the cross for our sins" picture of Jesus. Memories can be nails that build the future, or hurt in the now, or rust in place, losing their integrity.

In my first memory, I carry a bucket of nails. I carry them for myself, my father, our family, our future. We build our internal home with the memories we bring forward and learn to bring to language, and, in learning to speak them, we can release them and choose something new. This is the great gift of human creativity. We have been given the power, the tools, and the capacity to build our lives, to destroy our lives, to remodel our mind, to make new choices, and to refresh our interior architecture at any moment.

I hold the belief—formed from this memory—that for me to be valuable in a relationship, I need to be a worker, a hauler. My worth is based on proving my efficiency and strength while being of service.

> *If you can create a belief, and a belief can be that*
> *foundational, then you can uncreate the belief*
> *and change your whole world view.*

This uncreating and changing is what I call choice. I see now that I wanted to carry the bucket. The bucket is Lightyear. The tools are in the bucket. It is a blessing. I have a choice. I can carry the bucket because I carry the bucket. I do not need to load it with so much meaning. Unless, of course, I want to, and then I can, for fun and interest.

I can put the bucket down. I can empty the bucket. I can ask my dad to carry it. Infinite interpretation.

My father begins early on entrusting me with that bucket of nails, knowing I will help architect the companies and organizations and lifestyles of the future. In my first nine years, he's taught me to carry nails, fix and prime a well pump, clear sludge from a septic tank, build electric fences, push a cow from behind, dig out dried mud cake from the hot water heater room, and run cable down the cliff.

Does my father say to me, "Suzy, I entrust you with the future. Would you like to invent the next generation of Gablin Gift of the Gab Gizmos?" No, he does not. I say that. I am the keeper of the interpretation of my memories—both the ones I directly recall and the ones I directly recall being told to me about me. I offer this: What are the stories told about you? What are your earliest memories? If they do not support the person you choose to be today, reinterpret the memories. What have you made them mean?

Taking a ferry to school twice a day, I begin to picture our car careening off the ramp and into the dark waters swirling with kelp many times. I share this fear with my dad, and he has me visualize being successful in an emergency. I think through how to escape a car that drives into the water, equalizing the pressure by rolling down the windows and swimming out.

Going to bed, I face this fear of drowning in the car and picture the slow roll of my hands on the window handles, the calm holding of the breath, and the swimming free. I now see, through this picture of rolling the windows open, that I revitalized choice in being an emergency C-section birth. I swim free and take my first breath. We have the power to convert any fear into a positive picture of action that allows us to find opportunity in the danger. The inner voice commands: "Show me how to escape and free myself." This is the voice-activated reality, unlocking life.

By age five, I know that the square root of four is two, and twenty-five is five. By age six, I can open Heinekens. In a few years, at age thirteen, I'll be able to talk rudimentary nuclear fission with scientists that will visit our home, and by age sixteen, I'll master nuclear talk and drinking Heinekens at the same time. Life skills for a young woman entering the workforce in the early eighties.

Meanwhile, back at the birthday table outside of Chicago, C-section stories are finished, candles blown out, Dad has called from wherever he is to wish me a happy birthday, and above us, the *Apollo* 11 astronauts are approaching their target of the Moon. Images of Earth seen from space—bright and alive against the darkness and mystery—impress deeply on my subconscious through the live broadcast. There for us all to see fully: our mother, Gaia.

All people born after 1969 have grown up with a picture of our gorgeous planet Earth from space seen by humans standing on the Moon. It takes traveling to the Moon to see the Earth; taking the risk to land in another place to see home fully and to appreciate its beauty. Such is the realm of memory and choice. Our life memories are precious and powerful and help us take the risks to further the adventure.

What foundational beliefs about your childhood, your mother, your father, your siblings, your ethnicity, socio-economic status, body type, education, etcetera, can you call into question? Imagine yourself on the Moon, viewing yourself far away on Earth. Look at these established beliefs from a starry vantage point in space for greater perspective, so that you will not feel so defined by them.

3

Liberate Beauty

Vashon Island, Washington
Two years earlier
Fall 1967

Dad has been experimenting with various types of polyresins—goopy, viscous, air-hardening substances that have uses beyond my understanding of world commerce. The Saturday morning of the sea creature preservation project goes something like this:

Ever-present fog lifts just a touch higher off the horizon line as I look out the window across the Sound to Gig Harbor. Dory rolls over in our bed and greets me. "Hey, Slug." She pushes her thick, short, auburn-brown bangs out of her hazel-green-streaked eyes, revealing the sparkle of an untold plot steeping, her mind preparing for a life-or-death adventure—a bushwhack treasure hunt along the water's edge at high tide.

I turn from the window, lying face to face with Dory and her invitation, our heads on floral-print Merimekko pillowcases, her brown mass and my blonde mass, the difference of recombinant DNA and the sameness, breathing each other's exhales. At only nine years old, Dory's cheekbones are high, she is tall and strong and slender— an athlete in the making— shooting past all height norms known to man, her olive skin even and welcoming. I am soft, thick, and clumsy and am told so. "Suzy has weak thumbs." "Suzy has flat feet." Mom has to choose outfits for me from the "chubby" sizes in the Sears catalog. I am "Slug."

Heat radiates from the metal grate wrapping the entire central internal steel chimney that warms our Island home, chill entering the top of our heads as degrees escape out the single-pane window behind our pillows. A touch of woodsmoke rises along with waffle and sausage smells from the spiraling staircase, evidence that Dad is awake and at work on breakfast. Dory looks inside me, assessing my capabilities for the task ahead. She already knows my willingness.

"Wanna help me find creatures?"

YES! I resound without speaking, my head nodding and my wide seven-year-old eyes jet-streaming "YES" from my very optic nerve and core of my being. Bounding out of bed, I forage for shorts and a t-shirt in the vast communal closet. Our dresser has no boundaries of clear ownership—stripes and polyester are strewn about everywhere.

Our home is built on a piece of land that Dad has secured from erosion in the front by commissioning a double-level bulkhead built from enormous basalt boulders. The A-frame is established a modest, yet monumental, twenty feet above the high-tide line. Stone steps are fashioned from the house level to the lower level eight feet down, where the flagpole flies the American flag. We raise and lower the flag as a family daily. My father is an Eagle Scout and a reluctant Korean War draftee, and as the Vietnam War wages its own erosion of the American soul, our flagpole clangs in the wind, sounding my father's personal patriotic commitment. Another set of rock steps leads from the flagpole level to the beach itself. Thirty feet or so of barnacle-covered beach stretches out past the bulkhead and then, at low tide, a strip of sandy beach is revealed and slips under the sea.

Behind the house, we are not secured from erosion, as mudslides in Western Washington are part of living. During long rainy seasons, the gravel and dirt cliff behind the A-frame slides, leaving us with a giant hill to play on for months, until we can hire an earth mover to clear it.

"The tide is out!" Dory declares after getting a good look, thinning fog revealing the edge of the water and the sand.

"How far?" I ask, pulling on hot-pink terry stretch shorts and a matching top with neon yellow stripes. Even though it is September, and school has begun, the air is summer warm, almost seventy degrees.

"To the drop-off," she says with command and conviction.

TO THE DROP-OFF. My heart sinks and soars simultaneously. The deep mystery of the drop-off . . . the place where the waters pull themselves back so far that they reveal the slope of smooth eelgrass. In the drop-off, anything is possible. Most of our exploits on the beach are on the barnacled rocks, our feet scantily clad with flip-flops as we search for baby crabs and find the occasional tiny eel, uncovering the interacting worlds underneath each rock as we roll it away with our combined strength. At low tide, the sandy beaches present themselves with geoduck necks and razor clams and fields of sand dollars and moon snails. Limpets, muscles, and oysters encamp permanently on the rocks, dependent on the tides to bring them the salty water and microscopic food.

I grasp the wrought-iron railing of the spiral stairs with my right hand, stepping fast down the clockwise turn, spinning into the living room past the Danish couch and into the kitchen with the centrifugal force of a hot-pink golf ball twirling home in the last hole of a mini-golf course. These are the stairs I fell down as a toddler, with no memory of my own save the bump on my nose where I am told it broke.

Dad is facing the kitchen counter with his wide back to me, one I rode on in the water many times as a three-year-old learning to swim while he swam breaststroke style strong and steady, an island of personal power unto himself—me with arms around his neck. This is my own memory, while the stairs and my nose are a recounting from others, yet, like the closet, the boundaries of self and other merge. He is opening the waffle maker, loosening the crispy thing with a fork. The task is easy, for the iron is primed with extra grease from the already-prepared sausages.

Racing past the primal olfactory call of melted butter on gluten anything, I grab my sea bucket, scrambling down the enormous basalt boulders that Walt, the only guy on the island with a Caterpillar forklift big enough to move rocks of this size, had built into a bulkhead to protect our home from winter storms.

Our feet are practiced at running, climbing, jumping, and fishing from the edges of these uneven boulders when the tide is high, waves slapping against the rocks. Yet on this Saturday morning, in the miracle of coinciding events called a low tide, the beach stretches before us, seaweed hissing in the morning air, blanketing the rocks and making them slippery, though the barnacles underneath the seaweed make a type of reverse crampon. My archless feet curve over the deep green stones, the jagged edges of the barnacles coming up through the seaweed, giving me just enough grip to not slip.

After navigating the strip of rocky beach, I run over the thread of sandy beach with speed and ease, to the rare and unpredictable drop-off. Early morning, windless, the flat surface of the water becomes a window like no other. Many feet down, I see adult fish of myriad species moving with rare confidence, as if they know I cannot reach them in the deep, only see them. Flounders, a type of flat fish, typically camouflaged against the sandy bottom, stand out strikingly against the waving streamers of eel-grass, their two eyes twisted upward, slim flat bodies undulating, pulsing through the water, slipping under grass and becoming invisible again. I can see starfish against the green also, and Dungeness crabs large enough to eat. Everything in the drop-off is grown up, unlike the tiny miniature versions Dory and I find in our rock-rolling exploits.

"Come here!" Dory calls with the authority that a sibling two years and two months older is granted by the unspoken rules of incarnation order.

Dory has found something important. I don't need to ask as I turn my head over my shoulder. I can see in the way she is squatting over a group of stones in the transition between the barnacle band and the sandy strip, her left hand cupped, her right forefinger touching gently her discovery. Much of living on the water and walking the beaches is non-verbal. Often the distance and the sounds of the waves, gentle though they often are, make shouting unworkable. I learn to scan the horizon and movements and hand signals, my mother standing on the precipice of the bulkhead waving us in for a meal, or circling a beach towel with one arm like a lasso to tell us to get out of the water, or my father lifting a shovel overhead to let us know he has found a good place for clamming. All of these silent signals mean "come here."

She likely knows I am captivated by the uncommon sights of the drop-off and therefore initiates voice-control. Backing out of the water I have waded into, like a scuba diver backs out of the surf heels first with long fins following, I reach the semi-solid shore, pivoting, flip-flops slapping the back of my heels, wheezing as water is pressed out of them with each step. Muddy, life-rich sand spits onto the back of my legs, the suction of the rubber to the wet sand adding to the effort needed to arrive by Dory's side. I squat beside her.

This I have never seen.

A creature with thin arms waving energetically, as Dory has enough water in her cupped hand to give this being a touch of its liquid environment. In the small pool of her hand it seems to "wave swim" with its arms, and when an arm comes out of the water it sticks to the muscle of her thumb and rests. Or did it not have the energy to move when out of the water? I cup some clear saltwater from the pool and refill her hand, the creature now free again in the deep of her personal ocean. It spins and waves like a starfish, yet no starfish we have ever seen moves like this.

With still no words between us, my sandy knee touching hers, Dory lifts her head towards our plastic bucket. Welcoming my task, I grasp the white plastic part of the bucket handle and run back to the edge, kicking up as much sand mud as before. Taking care not to slip on the already slippery seagrass, I steady myself in a sumo-type stance, throw the bucket out before me with both hands, and pull it back towards me with the fresh saltwater rushing in.

This is an adult-sized bucket. I have seen the "summer people" and their "summer children" with child-sized toy sand buckets on the beach. My parents have us work with real tools. There are no child-sized buckets—there is simply life.

I learn young to carry more than I know how, strengthening myself.

Dory and I are Islanders attending school off island, yet we're certainly not "summer people." Summer people own vacation homes to escape from their mainland lives and visit perhaps a few weekends over the year. They miss out on the dark, wet winters with fires in the hanging hibachi, the clams roasted in sand pits, and the dusting of snow on the seashore. In their pursuit of comfort, they miss the autumnal tides and drop-off. They miss the discovery that awaits those willing to attempt living on a seven-mile-long island without a bridge connecting it to the mainland, without recognizable television reception or restaurants serving anything beyond the Brazier Burger, where you might build a boat motor from a Sears-and-Roebuck kit, with only your nuclear family to entertain you.

The summer people do not know what they are missing!

I carry my bucket back the way I secured the seawater: two hands in front of me, knees slightly bent, walking side to side, sloshing seawater and bits of seaweed onto the insides of my knees and terry shorts as I traverse the barnacle field, an eager child soldier of big and uncertain living, and arrive beside my sister.

Dory has covered the creature with her right hand and submerges both hands in the bucket, opens them slowly, and places each hand on the side of the bucket, now stable on a patch of flat sand. Together we witness the full movement of the creature, spinning and waving its arms to move with tremendous agility; the very tiniest tips of its arms carrying out the last touch of a wave with flourish. Her catch rests on the bottom and then, unprovoked—and believe you me, Dory and I were master provokers; when we wanted to see something move, we would poke it, rock the bucket, do whatever it took—it spun-swam again around its half-bucket of water, returning to settle motionless on the bottom.

"What is it?" I ask as only a little sister can, with full faith that my older sister knows the answer. Dory knows everything. She knows the ferry schedule backwards and forwards, the Tahlequah (Island) and Point Defiance (Tacoma) sides, the bus numbers and the transfer locations, my dad's office phone number; she knows how to get in for free at the Point Defiance Aquarium to feed Gus, the sea otter. When we have lots of extra time on the Tacoma side of our commute after just missing a ferry, Dory knows how to make games out of kicking rocks and pine cones to entertain us over our long daily journeys, and how to survive on twenty-five cents of sunflower seeds purchased from the drug store at the Downtown Tacoma transfer point. She knows how to call my mom from the pay phone on the Island side without using a dime, how to fix roller skates, and how to make "chocolate milk" out of muddy water to sell at our "store" where we use specially selected beach rocks for money. She knows how to make different voices for each stuffed animal on our bed—foreign accents, boy voices, girl voices, non-human tropical jungle animal voices, secret agent voices, alien voices, and teacher voices.

As children of an entrepreneur and inventor, Dory and I have learned that when we don't know something, there is no reason to be concerned, because we can make it up. This is why, with full confidence and authority, speaking into my faith-filled ears, Dory declares, "Slug, it's a star swimmer." She does not bat a lash.

"Mmm . . . ," I reply to Dory's knowledge—to the wisdom of the person who so aptly named the star swimmer, as it was both like a starfish yet could swim.

"Let's take it up to Daddy," she says.

Carrying our bucket together side by side across the bands of sand and barnacles, up the bulkhead rocks, it is easy to do together, feeling safer and wiser with my sister. Water sloshes from the edges of our bucket as we lift it up onto the large outdoor table by the house where Dad has set up a series of glasses with resin used to create the small, puck-like creature collection. Along the edge of the table are the completed specimens so far: a chiton, a few limpets of varying size, a small rock crab, a bright orange starfish, a baby oyster, and a small set of barnacles and purple muscles. The pungent smell of active resin overtakes me, a shift from the strong signal of drying seaweed at low tide. My feet are covered with muddy sand, my nostrils now filled with another world, one from inside the minds of men—powerful, productive, fantastic. It's 1967 and we are experiencing "The Wonderful World of Chemicals." Investments made by the titans of the military-industrial complex are now paying off, wartime inventions are being popularized via public relations advertisements, and school lessons normalize the use of insecticides and chemical fertilizers. The use of plastics is expanding along with the introduction of polyester in clothing, accommodating the growth of American waistlines resulting from more processed foods preserved with chemicals and additives, spun like cotton candy with the magic of ad men.

I experience the active resin right in my nose. Sweet, seductive, deadly, life-giving, transformative.

Dory lifts her star swimmer. "Look, Daddy," she implores, holding her hands up together to secure the treasure and give him a good look.

With large blue eyes sparkling behind horn-rimmed glasses and the wide heart of a father, he says, "Well, look at that! What have you got there?" His voice is deep, distinctive, and electric, made so by the infinite flow of ideas within his own mind.

"It's a star swimmer," Dory replies. I nod beside her. She is tender with it, observant, and captivated. Her gaze remains right there within her hands, holding the living being and its environment all in one. The fleetingly protective containment of her hands lets small drops of seawater escape down her arms in rolling beads. She is in love with both the creature and her task.

My father can sweat even in cold weather. He worked farms and fields as a boy in Illinois, read every book in his hometown library, built his own radios with his father at the end of World War II, became a lifeguard, played basketball, went to college on a football scholarship, and, while living in the state of Washington, became quite an accomplished downhill skier. At six feet, his legs are surprisingly short, and his long torso holds the lungs of a champion athlete. Sometime when I was around two, he underwent a triple-fracture skiing accident that immobilized him for many months. As the family story goes, that was the beginning of a long and slow progression of changes in his body, habits, and lifestyle that will ultimately lead to an experimental intestinal bypass surgery at Vanderbilt University for morbid obesity.

Turning from the array of sea creature specimens and setting aside his internal wheels of invention and calibrating formulas and processes, his drops of sweat land in Dory's handheld micro aquarium—seawater to seawater.

"Grrrrreat, Tiger!" he barks in congratulatory enthusiasm, with the same "Rrrr" in "Great" like Tony the Tiger of Kellogg's Frosted Flakes says it. His voice is always louder than it needs to be. Mom figures artillery training at Fort Bliss may have left him a touch deafened. Our father calls us both by the nickname of Tiger, but we know who he is talking to by the way he speaks, just as when my mom calls us "Baby" and we know who she is addressing.

"You know the drill." Now part-teacher, scientist, and Eagle Scout. "Get your specimen as dry as possible before we put him in."

Dory is practiced in her project, having already encased the chitons and such on the table. They have hardened—"cured" is the technical term—and have turned ever so slightly yellow orange. The surfaces and depths of the discs are varied, reflecting the morning diffused light, and the tiny rock crab one has bubbles sealed within it from the hand crafting of the process or the crab's hopeless escape attempts, or both.

Dory hesitates and brings her hands now close to her body. I look over her elbow at the creature, the water level slowly lowering in her palm. We rushed from the beach to share the discovery, yet now, facing the momentum of her school project, there is a churning, a pivoting, a nurturing, a rebellion, a pleasing, an alchemical mixture of forces both within and without acting on her, catalyzing action. She scans the shoreline with the possible question: Do I release the star swimmer or go forward?

No words are exchanged. A type of choice is in the making—the choice of momentum, of finishing what one begins, of follow-through, of what we are taught. Contrasted with the conflicting choice to reverse the embalming process and release the creature, Dory proceeds.

The star swimmer on a Glad paper towel, wicking the sea-water from its tiny little fingerlike tendrils, lifts an arm with great effort, reaching for home, the Sound, the water, the pool underneath the rock. It stretches out and falters back onto the paper. Another finger-arm thingy, more wet than the other, begins the dance again, and with strength from its center begins to turn slightly, a feat of extraordinary agility. Dory gently dabs it with an open edge of the paper towel, with the love of a mother and the precision of a scientist, just enough to absorb the excess water, the star swimmer settling, resting, dying—one cannot be sure.

Impulsively, I touch it with my chubby wet forefinger to know more, to be part of the process, to be close to the star swimmer, and my sister and my father. Water runs off my finger to its fingery appendage, the droplets enlivening it, the tendril pulsing off the Glad paper towel.

"Ugh, Sue, no!" Dory reprimands, stern and quiet.

I snatch my hand, tucking it behind my lower back as if the impulse could be better restrained from there.

"Now I have to dry it again!" Of course I knew that as soon as

I did it, yet the timing of realization and regret hasn't yet synchronized in my young mind. Daddy . . . or is it Dad? My first year at Annie Wright I realized the other girls referred to their parents as Mom and Dad, while Dory and I call them Mommy and Daddy. We are Baby or Tiger, and I am Slug to Dory. All this makes sense in a home where everyone sleeps in the same room, on a pile of rocks overlooking a beach where colonies of creatures live closely under and on top of rocks.

Here at home, he is Daddy, and at school I've begun the judicious and hardening task of growing up—of learning how to call Daddy "Dad."

"Ready?" Daddy asks.

Dory nods and uses her right hip to push me an inch or two and uses two toothpicks to lift the star swimmer. She begins to place it on the surface of the liquid resin my father has prepared, awaiting gravity to pull it downwards and into the center. The substance is liquid enough that the star swimmer responds as if in water, a return to its home element, a finger wrapping around the toothpick, making it hard to place it within the shallow glass. Dory gets all the limbs in and begins to arrange them with her tip of the toothpick, but the star swimmer is far more dynamic than the mussels or chiton of last weekend's harvest. An arm is now out of the mixture; two out, and the resin is setting, thickening faster than time. Dory adjusts by moving the center a bit, and a tip sticks to the edge of the glass as one of the star swimmer's arms breaks, while the other continues the fated reach out of the resin.

Distraught, Dory begins to align the broken arm bit with the main body to rescue the symmetry of the specimen with her remaining moments of plasticity. My father watches intensely, the teller, not the doer, of deeds. By this time, my father has solidly begun the path to morbid obesity, although none of us has that specific language for it at the time. His fingers do not have the quick dexterity of Dory or me, and we both know he cannot save this project from the gummy, bubbly entombment it is becoming.

Exhaling the two-part epoxy of the delight of her discovery and the tragedy, Dory calls it, saying, "This one is over." She takes her toothpicks and sets them into the mostly hardened mixture, straight up like mini flag-poles marking the micro grave.

I learn many years later that our star swimmer is indeed a brittle star. Witnessing the grace and agility of its movement in Dory's hands and then in my adult-sized bucket, I know I have been in the presence of *life*. In our zeal to capture the moment and preserve our discovery, the broken body of the star swimmer is encased, yet the beauty escapes.

Human beings to me are star swimmers, and in our free and natural state, we are beautiful.

Beliefs and worldly expectations are like the two-part
resin epoxy that encases this natural state, and we
must find a way to free ourselves.

I understand that the metaphor does not extend perfectly, yet you see, yes? What is our natural state? What is our place in the family of things? What if we could be ourselves and swim among the stars? What if that requires seeing through the clear resin hardened and set up around us to pull ourselves out? Questions are the tool to liberate our beauty.

I begin a journey on this day with the star swimmer, becoming less and less the full potential of myself, more hardened to the world; losing flexibility with every math test I score 100 on and losing choice with every rope I am too weak to climb, losing confidence each time an adult tells me I am a leader instead of me knowing that for myself, labeled and pasted on the plywood: "Susanne is [fill in the blank]." All this by the beginning of second grade, with no egregious villain in sight.

Just as Michelangelo claims to have liberated the statue of David from the stone, we can liberate ourselves from the resin, from the inside out, and release all that is not ours, allowing the stone to fall away and the beautiful self to swim free.

4

"Communicate, Goddammit."

Sun City, Arizona

Summer 1973

The dull sound of the air conditioner switches on in my grandparents' Sun City, Arizona, home as my Grandpa Larson—a fixture on the couch—is watching the live, televised Watergate hearings. My mother and grandmother have successfully negotiated funds from my grandpa to purchase a new living room set. This one has an extra-long couch, known as a davenport, with a matching love seat. Gramma Larson has style and tremendous personal energy, which is reflected in her choice of a satin, shiny blue and green brocade upholstery—cool to sit on and easy to clean, yet we are not allowed to eat on it or even have food near it.

The extra-long design makes for a great place to take a nap—all part of the master plan, as Gramma rises at five a.m. to bake and avoid "heating up the place." By two p.m., she is ready for a nap. All that has changed now, due to the excruciatingly slow and extended Watergate hearings. President Nixon is unrequited in his innocence, while members of the Republican Party are on trial and providing testimony. Little do I know I am witness to some of the first "reality TV shows." My Grandpa Larson would rather be keelhauled than miss an "episode," many of which last hours and hours on end, with nary a conclusion and zero comic relief.

"Thank God Congress doesn't hold hearings," Gramma says, "when it's time for *Wheel of Fortune* and *Jeopardy* to come on!" With her new napping spot displaced by Grandpa and his favorite "show," she's come into the extra bedroom where Dory and I have been staying. I like watching her nap. Body strong and thin, she walks every day and learned to swim at age sixty. "Girls weren't taught to swim in my day," she says, sharing a fact that has no file folder in my brain. Living on an island, it is unimaginable to me that anyone would not know how to swim.

Lying on her back, with her ankles crossed and her arms across her chest, and her eyes closed, she appears asleep, though I know she is not. She does not sleep during these naps. She must have invented something better than sleep. I can tell when she is actually asleep by how she breathes and holds her mouth. I know these things because over the years, my mother has said to my sister and me, "Don't wake up your gramma! Let her rest, for God's sake." Of course, this has led me to watch her nap patterns carefully in order to recognize even the slightest stirring, so that I can thereby avoid violating the "don't wake up" clause.

My grandparents are lifestyle leaders of their Chicago-based friend and family group, selling their Palos Park, Illinois, brick ranch home and moving to the new Del Webb "active retirement" development of Sun City in the fall of 1969. Each summer, my parents send Dory and me to stay with them for an extended period, sometimes as long as three to four weeks, and this has continued now that they live in the Southwest.

I am twelve, almost thirteen years old, a woman-child, now 5 feet 10 inches tall. Dory is six feet tall and competing at the state level in shotput and the javelin. We are often mistaken by lecherous men as adults, or perhaps I am giving these "searching for Lolita" types too much credit. Suffice it to say, how I see myself and how the world of men sees me are two very different things. I am deeply uncomfortable with the amount of "attention" I receive. The safe stuff is the whistling and catcalling from the landscapers hired to trim the infinite amount of ornamental orange trees with their white-painted trunks planted throughout the development. When Dory and I ride our bikes, baskets filled with pool towels and flip-flops, unescorted by Gramma, we might as well be on a catwalk in a stripper bar as we pass the tree trimmers and palm choppers.

I look over at Gramma, her eyes still closed.

"Gramma, can we go to the pool now?" Stillness. Chest rising.

"Gramma, can I get out the paints on the porch?" Stillness. Chest falling.

Going for the one that always works: "Gramma, want to play three-deck rummy?" Her left eye opens slightly. A gamer at heart, I always have her at "play."

Three-deck rummy, as I learned it from Gramma, is an interesting game of chance, skill, and visual patience. Three entire decks of cards are mixed, minus the Jokers (thank you), and each player is dealt five cards. You draw from the deck until you can make a three-card play—three of a kind or three in a row—and then as the game continues each player can add and borrow from these growing sets of options as long as there is a minimum of three cards in the play. With three decks, the volume of patterns increases, and the more watchful and creative I become, the more often I can win.

I watch my Gramma nap and she watches me play three-deck rummy. We watch each other with insight. Like the distributed energy grids of today or interconnected computer networks—the power of optimization—we rearrange for all to see, what already exists, into new patterns. The same cards are there on the table, and yet for the person who can *see*, they play all their cards by connecting what is already there by making something new from what already is.

You see, unlike poker, three-deck rummy is a game you win by getting as many cards as possible visible and on the table, for all to see. It is a game of rearranging, finding place and pattern instead of playing things "close to the chest." You win by playing all your cards and going "out."

The Watergate testimonies continue, and even though it is the height of daylight—rather, actually for that reason, so as not to "work the air too hard, mind you"—all the shades and curtains are drawn, the living room darkened, and my grandfather's permanently frowning face is illuminated by the bluish light of the TV.

Dory has inherited the deeper streak of intellectualism from my parents' union, both of them masterful varsity debaters in college. Her mind bright and engaging, and having completed her third year at Charles Wright Academy, she is trained to question. "Nixon knows everything," Dory says, walking from the extra bedroom in front of Grandpa and for a moment cutting off the light from the TV as she makes her way to the other end of the extra-long couch.

Grandpa doesn't take his eyes off the set.

"He's working hard to cover it all up," she says as a second note to draw his attention.

Today—July 16—Alexander Butterfield testifies live and reveals that, for two years, there has been an extensive secret taping system in the White House and that Nixon has been recording all the goings and comings in his office. This is *big* news and Dory knows it. There *is* evidence; it's just a matter of time and how to get it. As little kids, when asked, "What do you want to be when you grow up?" I would passionately describe my benign future as "a mommy and a dancer!" Dory, with calm intelligence, would always say, "A secret agent." She would stump me with how vastly cool and worldly she is.

She is learning to play a different game than three-deck rummy.

I am learning that some conversations are in the open and some are secret. I begin to learn that the open ones have more solutions.

"What about that secret taping system, Grandpa?"

"Well, you got me there, Butch," he replies without looking at her, nodding slightly as if he is conceding and not up for a fight. "Butch" is his nickname for all his five grandchildren, and Dory is his eldest. The word is gender and age neutral.

Dory pivots. "Looks like a lot of old white guys. When do you think Blacks will be in office?"

His eyes lift from the TV to her. He chuckles. "Never."

She knows she's got him now. "What do you mean never? Of course they will. Have you been watching all the things happening across the Midwest?"

"Yes, I have, and I don't like it one damn bit."

"Well, that's why they had to have the Civil Rights Act, because people like you would never change and you—"

"No law can make me like the coloreds," he says, his voice rattling with a bit of phlegm.

"My point exactly," Dory slings back from her end of the couch.

Gramma inhales deeply, the kitchen table covered with cards. I am looking for a place to play a three of hearts. She gets up to bring Grandpa ice water and shoots my sister a look I cannot see yet feel as Dory replies to her, eyes half smiling, "Gramma, how can you put up with this man?"

Gramma radiates self-mastery, knowing her entrance into the living room has shifted the energy even if only for the moment, and replies, "You know, Dory, I chose him." Gramma has often told us the story of how handsome Grandpa was as a young man—a basketball player from a good family. He was a way out and up for her; she wanted him, and she got him, so she never complains. Ever.

We need each other in an odd and dislocating way. Dory confronting. Grandpa holding staunch to the old beliefs as they are giving way under the transformation of Civil Rights, women's rights, and a new beachhead within the presidency. Gramma prioritizes, directs, harmonizes, and of course, bakes. I pester them all, still playing like a child—swimming and going to mini-golf after the blazing summer Arizona sun retires to let the sidewalks radiate heat until the next morning.

There are many, many plays of three-deck rummy on the table in the world, ours and the larger one, turning evenly under the eyes of satellites. Gramma is the queen of hearts and Dory the jack of spades. Grandpa is the ten of diamonds and I am the two of clubs. Many cards still are in our hands, unplayed, unspoken, with the future unfolding.

Thomson, Illinois
August 1974

In a 1970 gold-colored Chevrolet Caprice, my mother, sister, and I, and our smooth-coated Saint Bernard dog, Brandy, travel cross-country to Thomson, Illinois, the childhood home of my father, to visit my other grandparents, Orville and Esther Gablin, known as Grampa and Gramma Gablin. We see them a lot less frequently for all the reasons that make sense, including the most basic one: They are my dad's parents.

With the tremendous power of dramatic foreshadowing, my mother's driving becomes more aggressive as we approach town. My father always says she drives like a Puerto Rican cab driver. We are now officially moving from Vashon to Louisville, Kentucky, where my dad will work for PPI, Protective Packaging, Inc., a company of his own creation that has several patents on transportation systems for low-level radioactive waste. He perfected the designs while we lived on the island, using the time walking on the beach at low tide to envision new solutions. To test some of his prototypes at high temperature, he once put the oven on self-clean and placed them inside. As he opened the door, a rush of oxygen caused a moderate explosion. My mother jested that some couples need separate bedrooms, but they need separate kitchens. When he experimented with different foam insulation delivery systems, he once used the blender that my sister and I learned how to make snow cones with by putting it on "shave" mode, and permanently destroyed it, gumming it up with mysterious coagulating agents of unknown origin. These are the losses we've borne, being children of an inventor and salesman.

In the process, I am slowly learning to become less sensitive, and it is unclear whether this is a positive or negative. It depends. What is clear is that I have learned how to hide while appearing to be present, looking stronger and wiser to the world while burying gifts that might betray my cover as a common apathic teen. I learn to become like a small octopus, fitting into new environments, into tiny irregular spaces, changing color, blending in.

Dory's sea creature display that has endured the last eight years is currently in prime secure transport in our very car versus the risky moving van, due to its intrinsic sentimental value.

Dad has a number of key sayings that have made it into his life playbook:

"There is a difference between scrap and junk."

"Something is better than nothing."

"No management through surprise."

"Communicate, goddammit!"

I name the long road trip "From Rock to Roll." The "Rock" is the unflattering nickname Mom has for Vashon Island, and "Roll" is because that is what we do in the permanent position of the backseat with a dog that outweighs you by five pounds, anytime we take a turn.

Rolllll.

My mother's hands are on the wheel at ten and two o'clock, her foot on the Chevy accelerator, pulsing slightly, perhaps a racing technique, a nervous habit, or a high-performance pattern, like when she reads and tilts her book back and forth ever so slightly, entering a flow state of consciousness. Rows and rows of corn hypnotically open their perpendicular aisles to my eyes looking out of the window.

Dory is hot, maybe depressed. I don't know because we don't talk about things like that. Her head rests on the passenger window, and I imagine she is finding ways to tolerate the changes ahead. She is sixteen, a driver in her own right, and the partner for my mother on this road trip, as my dad will fly and join us in Chicago. Her hair is thick and brunette with reddish highlights. Her skin is smooth and her mind steady, but she is leaving more behind than any of us: two years into high school, one of the most progressive on the West Coast, camping and sailing trips, advanced math and chemistry, track and field, music, and so, so, so many boys—yet they are not of interest to my sister nor her to them, at least not in that way. Dory has a broad, platonic friendship with all people and an unparalleled openness to race, gender, and size.

I sense Dory knows all of it better. Two years of age difference in siblings matters in world history when it is one-seventh or one-eighth of your life. Dory has had more direct contact with the kids that were seniors and properly part of the hippie generation of dissenters and social activists. Her blue couch debates with Grandpa Larson showcased her knowledge and cemented my belief that Dory was out to save the world and good at it. She knew about the Mekong Delta, Civil Rights, and racial violence. She knew how to name the star swimmer.

Mom slows to the town speed limit, more out of self-preservation than any form of inner rule-following. On Vashon, a speeding ticket was always published in the local paper, and let's just say Mom made "news" often. She is naturally suspect of all small towns, Thomson being no exception. The Chevy turns on to the gravel driveway beside Grampa Gablin's pick-up truck and camper, which is on cinder blocks next to the brambles of exploding raspberry bushes against the wooden fence.

"Okay, girls, get your stuff out of the back and take Brandy for a walk."

For the last four years, since I negotiated with my father to get the dog of my dreams, a Saint Bernard, after researching dog breeds in a tiny book called *Dogs of the World*, Brandy followed me as much as I followed her.

I open my door and Brandy—all 130 pounds of her—jumps over me to get out and begin the sniff assessment. Her wide jowls swing back and forth across the driveway and sidewalk with professional ease like a landmine sweeper or metal detector. She stops and looks up, having identified a key source of scent.

On the step in front of her is Gramma Esther Jackson Gablin with hands on her hips, a hand-sewn apron, a genetic frown that she rarely overcomes, and an unchanging, consistent unemotional demeanor coupled with an ever-working unpausing movement from domestic station to station that I later understand to be German.

Finding myself right behind my massive dog, there is no subtlety to our arrival, and I step up on the porch stairs to hug my grand-mother. A nanosecond of reflexive Germanic withdrawal is countered by a tender patting on my back.

"Well, you made it," she says, stating the obvious. These visits every two years give me a sense of how much has changed in my life and how little has changed in theirs. "Oh, and how are you?" she asks Brandy. "Look, you have grown too!"

It is now clear who Brandy has been gunning for as Grampa Gablin walks up along the side yard, likely from working in his garage, which is a rural temple of tools, in-progress pieces of furni-ture, radio electronics, and mason jars of watermelon pickles. His hands wear a smidgen of grease and he strides like an Olympic speed walker, his ball cap over his completely bald head. He first pats the hood of our car, as if to tell the Chevy itself "good job" for getting us here. He embraces me, solid and sinewy, pets Brandy, kisses my mom, and hugs Dory all in a single choreographed move of welcome and pure energy.

"Well, you made it!" An animated echo of Gramma's welcome.

Birds sing the next morning, their voices pouring industriously through the open, screen-less window, even before the early summer light. I am happy to wake up, as sleeping on the horsehair beds is, well . . . what is it? Weird. Is it the crunching sound of the matted hairs rubbing against each other as I roll from one side to another? The odd, organic smell of horsehair and time? The windless, water-saturated, Southern Illinois air that makes a clean person wake up feeling filmy? Even Dory, namer-of-the-star-swimmer, lover of language and speaker of many voices, has summed up the sleeping experience at our grandparents' as . . . well, weird. When experiences are completely out of reach for us to bring to words, the word "weird" is our fallback, and holds massive meaning until we can work out more facts or details.

We awake uncharacteristically early, and together clamber down the certainly-not-to-code stairs that are so steep, narrow, and hazardous they might as well be a ladder. In the kitchen, the center of it all, Gramma Gablin is making pickles, pouring vinegar into mason jars, and Grampa Gablin swoops us up before we can sit at the table and guides us to the truck. Just like in Arizona, if anything important needs to happen in the summer, it needs to happen before 7:30 a.m. We pile into the truck with me in the middle of the front seat. With my scooching hips to Grampa and knees to Dory, I do my best to make space for the stick shift, and we head out for the Mississippi River.

As life would have it, weird often follows weird, and we clamber into a flat-bottomed river skiff as the sun is rising. The creatures of the night peel away, making room for the creatures of the morning. Dragonflies circle above, alighting for heartbeats on lily pads. They fly double, mating mid-air, holding off on their aerobatics until the sun is up longer. The heads of red-eared sliders and snapping turtles are still and statuesque, on the lookout for breakfast.

Grampa deftly guides our craft, following a fishing line made of light rope that he has baited earlier, perhaps a day or two ago. The river is calm, the current steady, and the water is creamy coffee brown. He lifts a long, wooden pole, places it just ahead a few feet, connects with the muddy river bottom, then pulls the skiff forward gently, lifting the line and checking each hook to see if there is a catfish. We have done this before on other visits, yet I clearly do not have enough actual experience to be any good at it and my level of appreciation for catfish is so low that I am only dimly inspired, and sleepy to boot. The heat comes with the sun, which has now risen above the tree line on the river's edge. The dewy gold light catches in my right eye, making it harder for me to see the line in the water to grab with the long-handled hook.

There's one. Alive, but subdued by enduring the river and the hook.

Dory musters her inner fisherwoman, collaborating instinctively with Grampa and the line, the fish, the pole, and the skiff. Dinner is secured—bonked with the catfish bonker that is similar yet smaller than the ones we used on salmon and halibut—and secured in the cooler. The line produces many more catfish as we travel across the branch.

And what of the weird often following weird? Well, all of this authentic river fishing Dory and I can get behind, and we have enough knowledge of boats and lines to be contributors despite being sleep-deprived relocating teenagers. You be the judge of this: once home, Gramma Gablin takes the catfish fillets that have been cleaned and with a hand-cranking meat grinder makes them into *catfish burgers!* This is *weird*, and I must draw the line somewhere. By the mere look of the grinder, I swear off catfish burgers for this lifetime and into the next.

Or so we think.

Later, Dad arrives from Chicago to join us for the weekend to continue our road trip south from Illinois to Kentucky. After a dinner of guess what? *Catfish burgers!* After a dinner where I pass on the burgers and eat my body weight in homemade coleslaw, we settle into the living room to watch television.

Like all televisions in 1974, Grampa Gablin's reception is fortified by techniques both scientific and ritualistic—the forming of aluminum sails between the rabbit-eared antennas, the adjusting of their direction, or the subtle holding of one's mouth a certain way to reduce fuzz or maintain the vertical hold of the frame. Each technique is considered legitimate and family members are applauded for their creative attempts to make the picture as clear as possible. Sometimes an occasional flip, say every forty-five seconds or so, with a clear image is preferred over a stable image that is "snowy."

In our family, Dory and I are a team, and we have great success with foil lightly crunched about the antennas, preserving the surface area. Here we are, though, in the midlands, with an unfamiliar device. Clearly Grampa's TV tuning is above our pay grade, and touching anything could be sacrilegious, disrespectful, or both. Mind you, none of this is considered weird by anyone. Indeed, it is considered normal by all.

Grampa, a veteran telegraph communications officer for the railroad, has "the touch." A slight adjustment of the left rabbit ear brings alignment, stability, and a cheer from all of us. We are now seated in the various fancy chairs of the front room, which, like the beds, are also filled with horsehair. The heavy strand of world events emerging and circling the whole year, like a giant skein of yarn untangling with reports, recordings, and Congressional hearings, almost straightens out on live television.

Grampa, now with the reception optimized, flips between the three—well, if you count Public Broadcasting Service, four—channel choices, stays on ABC, touches the top of the set gently, and narrows his eyes. He then walks backwards to his front-room chair and keeps his focus on the TV set as if to say, "I am watching you, so behave."

Richard Milhous Nixon is addressing the country tonight. *Now what?* His caricatured face, animated a million times and ways, is imprinted on my adolescent brain; the voice, the voice matching the face: sullen and jowly. Both my parents, and my mother especially, volunteered at the voting polls when we lived on the island. I recall late nights as a very young child falling asleep under the check-in table near my mother's feet, her extra sweater wadded under my head for a pillow.

I get out of my horsehair chair and opt for dog hair, my hands together under my right cheek. I lay my head on Brandy's middle, the place she is used to being laid on. She is now four, her fierce and extended puppy stage fizzling out, surrendered to her deep DNA of being a human rescuer. No kegs of brandy (yes, that is how innovative I was as a dog-namer) around her neck as she digs me out of a Swiss avalanche and lies beside my frozen body, licking my face to revive me. Her rescue, like all great dogs of all breeds, is to provide a bubble of the *now*, an immediate unconditional sense of belonging, place, and purpose, rescuing their people from being buried in their own avalanches of the past or the future.

I enter the bubble, lying half on floor, half on dog, and Nixon is now sideways from my view.

He resigns. He quits before he gets caught.

The voice goes on, droning his own accomplishments, which are vast and potentially marvelous, yet Nixon is illuminating his ends to silently justify the means. Just as there is no escape from the oppressive summer night's heat, there is no relief, really. He resigns before he is impeached. No clear lines drawn. None of this is weird and all of this is normal. In our family, the premium is placed on clear and open communication in the now, even if there is no agreement. Here I learn that, for the president of the United States, lying is now normal.

Human language—the spoken, the unspoken, the ridged inhale, the slight movement of the hand, the flutter of an eyelid . . . all of it in its many forms—is the great ocean we all swim in. We are often unaware of this powerful environment we exist in, and create, simultaneously. Communication is grossly underrated as a field of massively important study in modern education. As people are surrounded by all forms of man-made media and spending less time in nature, they have less time in communion, where the real and true communication can happen.

The word *communicate* comes from the Latin meaning "to impart, to make common." What is most important for you to impart to the world, to make common and available to others? What is it that you want to be known for? My Gramma Larson encouraged me to experience the power of getting as many cards as possible out on the table in her game of triple gin rummy, as a means to both discover a solution and have a good time. What if "winning" in life entails playing all our cards, joining with others who are playing theirs, giving all our gifts, and imparting them into the common pile, with nothing held back? Imagine how this type of collective communication, with shared wisdom in the commons, could change the speed of generating possibility for solving scientific and social challenges.

5

Judge Not

Thomson, Illinois, to Louisville, Kentucky
August 1974

Gramma Gablin misses my cheek in an awkward goodbye hug and kisses my ear, her puckered lips wet and bristled. She sends us off with jars of watermelon pickles for my dad. The Chevy is loaded up and geometry is now switched to Dad driving, Mom navigating, and Dory, Brandy, and me in the backseat. We warp-speed out of this small, small town into small towns, into towns, and then onto the Interstate. As we reach escape velocity, now safe to speak her mind, my mother puts her hand on my dad's knee.

"Well, Ken, that wasn't too bad."

This is, of course, a huge win for my dad: bridging the worlds of rural and urban, sales and science, fact and story.

The whole country is bantering, whether at burger drive-ins, taverns, or on radio programs dissecting our history's first presidential resignation. We stop and buy a *Chicago Tribune* to keep the front page for posterity.

The drive from Illinois to Kentucky follows river and farmland. I am excited for a new life. The idea of walking or riding a bike or even driving a car to school without taking a ferry is mind-blowing. The mainland. I now would live on the mainland. The idea of new friends, sleepovers, dates with boys, art and music—all of it rolls in my mind as we roll through the gentle mounds growing mono-crops under blue skies with cumulus clouds. My mom has a beautiful and well-trained voice and she sings along with the radio, windows down from time to time to give the AC a rest, her voice audible yet blended with the rushing air. "Strawberry keeps on burning." She harmonizes with the chorus of Creedence Clearwater Revival from "Proud Mary."

Dory interjects, "Mom. That's not the line." Mom, unruffled by the feedback of reality, continues as her version of the lyrics must make sense to her. This pattern of sticking with one's own idea even if it is incorrect becomes a hallmark of Gablin family life. We all are aware of it yet unwilling to change and bend to facts. Mom traces the problem back to her mother-in-law, Gramma Gablin.

The story goes like this: When my dad went to first grade (in those days there was no kindergarten, much less preschool, or pre-preschool or prenatal flash cards), his teacher tested him on his colors. Yellow is yellow, blue is blue, green is green.

While holding up a black card, Dad replied, "That is dark brown."

The teacher said, "No, Kenneth, this is black."

"No, my mother says that is dark brown."

My father sustained his full conviction and a parent-teacher conversation ensued later that day, during which Gramma also identified black as dark brown.

The joke is that my grandmother's cookies are never burnt because they are never black. They are always only dark brown, which by definition makes them edible.

So the strawberry keeps on burning. Black is dark brown. Presidents don't lie. Clear lines of "what is what" are bending before my eyes like the very real illusions on *The Amazing World of Kreskin,* a current TV show profiling a popular and entertaining mentalist.

We come upon the Ohio River on the border of Indiana and Kentucky. Massive and muddy. In my mind, it is filled with either toxins or leeches or both. These are the natural TV show biases of a fourteen-year-old who has only ever swum in saltwater and has watched a few too many nature documentaries.

The vibration produced by driving over the grated metal expanders built within the bridge for freezing and thawing rumbles through my feet rhythmically—*juop . . . juop . . . juop . . . juop*—then stops. We arrive on the Kentucky side and pull into a gas station to fill up. The gas shortages and resulting long lines of the early 1970s are beginning to ease, and self-service has been introduced, so Dory and I swap turns filling up the car and washing the windshield. Brandy jumps over me and out the door for a walk with Mom, Dory reaches for the gas pump nozzle, and I am searching for the bug-scrubber squeegee when two men get up from the green, woven lawn chairs at the front of the station and amble towards us.

The taller one comes to the front of the car and reaches across, a loose sleeve dragging in the washing fluid. "Hey, darlin', that there is my job, ya hear?" His tone is both ominous and superficially welcoming.

The second man arrives beside Dory. "Yip, 'n this one's mine."

Dory and I exchange baffled glances at their accents and willingly surrender our tasks, gliding off to the grass-covered strip where Brandy is divining a place to pee. Brandy eventually secures perfection and pees as only a Saint Bernard can: seemingly forever.

We rejoin the family back at our now clean and filled car, hop back in—a panting dog between Dory and me—and Mom passes back a Tab. Dad rolls up the windows, blasts the AC, which, since the engine has been off, is actually hotter than the ambient air, places his right arm along the back of the front seat, and with a partial spinal twist to get eyeshot of us, says:

"If you *ever* talk like that, I will cut your goddamned tongues out."

Dory and I give each other a look that says, "Well, that was intense and clear," our eyebrows up our faces. It is clear that my dad has a strong bias and opinion that sauntering accents are bad and should not be developed, no matter how long our exposure to this new culture will be. I must keep something clear in this murky swirling summer, so I decide to never become like "them," whoever "them" is.

> *As an adult, I can better discern and process the impact*
> *of strong emotion, either mine or another's, even when*
> *the opinion is slung like a hand grenade.*

In this moment, all I know is to stay in the backseat and be quiet. Across the river, and through the woods, to Louisville Kentucky Country Day School we go.

Louisville, Kentucky
November 1974

Fall arrives and school begins. We are somewhat settled into our new home, set on a grassy hill of four acres of lawn that needs to be mowed, with a creek winding through the front. When we first looked for homes, I fell in love with this one because of the creek. I felt the stream could be my bridge from one world to another, yet on an early exploration of my very own personal stream, I spied a water moccasin swimming menacingly, and I became hesitant to delight in the nature of the South. I have not grown up with this creek and do not trust its muddy, non-transparent waters and ways.

Most baffling is the daily violence, large and small, regarding forced busing. My parents have enrolled Dory and me in the Louisville Kentucky Country Day School, a private school where we will be sheltered from the aftermath of the Civil Rights Act. Yet there is no shelter. The daily local news is filled with bus burnings, protests, enraged TV interviews, people running from each other, flaming crosses, KKK white-hooded characters, and the bumpy camera work I've grown up with from Vietnam coverage, which brings the sense of attack, peril, and harm leaking through the television and onto the floor of our family den, where all television is watched.

Meanwhile, I have become acutely aware of the spectrum of Southern accents I hear. The Lohhhlaville, the Louey-Ville, and the swallowed syllables sung from thick-tongued speakers remind me of my father's edict never to sound like them, and yet here I am beginning the fall of my freshman year of high school, wanting to find my place and find friends. All of them speak some version of English just like the men three months ago that pumped gas for us on the Kentucky side of the Ohio River.

Enrolled in challenging courses—World Civilization, French II, Advanced Algebra, Chemistry, English Literature, and Fine Arts—I begin to feel the weight of homework, no friends, and new surroundings—or is it something else? At Charles Wright, I was second in my class in terms of GPA and was accustomed to doing well in school without having to study hard. Maybe it is the challenge of high school, adding in basketball and art when my advisor counseled me not to, or simply loneliness, but I can now see that I was suffering from the aftermath of judgment. I did not yet have any of those distinctions at that age, yet I had all the symptoms and heartache that come with being righteous. My new home gave me so many opportunities.

The water is brown.

Black people get yelled at.

They can never be president.

People talk funny.

I get reprimanded to not sound like them.

Women stay quiet.

There are no mountains or ocean.

Barbara pushed my hand into a banana cream pie at lunch.

Creeks have poisonous snakes.

There are lots of mosquitos.

Dad's boss is an alcoholic.

Mom smokes two packs a day.

Dad sweats so much he walks around in underwear.

My heart piles up micro and macro judgments, sentencing myself to a life of misery among the racist, drawl-speaking, mud-wading souls that I am trying to distance myself from. I am swallowed whole by myself. The snake with its own tail down its throat, the circle of judgment, suffocating and tight on my young heart now hardening. Who do the young call on for help in the midst of what everyone says is normal adolescence?

Gone is the Suzy who walks along the ferns, counting orange and clear jellyfish from the deck of the ferry in the spring when the water warmed and the dogwood bloomed. She has been replaced by an "upgraded" mainland version of West Coast undiagnosed elitism; a consciousness cleared to condemn the people around me without due justice in the name of "I know better."

Yet I don't, and neither do you.

Ouch! My distain for Louisville directs me to "I-Am-Above-You Land."

People ask me, "Where are you from again? Where is that?" As if Washington is so far away that it's floated off the map, or maybe we are only counting counties in Kentucky, not any states beyond. These Kentucky families have deep, multigenerational roots and cousin systems that extend and fork and branch across time. I am no match for the whiskey makers of lore, the great-grandchildren of circus inventors, the factorial snobbery, the debutante balls, the gowns, the Kentucky Derby, the mint juleps, the cheese grits, the confused expectation of the collapse of the antebellum South, and the new reality of the law of the land. And the twisters, which are not uncommon in Kentucky. Tornadoes. Swirling powers of the wind and heat, lifting things up into the air only to throw them down harshly and in another county. Displacement. Dislocation. Dis.

Dis ain't what I thought.

World Civilization is first period. In a midi-skirt, turtleneck, and calf-high boots, I stride in and take a seat near the door. My backpack lands beside me, the heft of *Civilizations through the Ages, Modern Mathematics,* and *Wuthering Heights* permanently sloping my left shoulder. Our teacher, Dr. Worthin, is a fan of impromptu in-class essays. I wonder if he delights in the collective groan of the class as he announces our topic for this morning by writing it in cursive on the chalkboard and saying each word as it is expelled from both the spittle in his mouth and the chalk in his hand in a flourish: COMPARE AND CONTRAST ROMAN SLAVERY TO AMERICAN SLAVERY.

Martha is at the desk beside me. She is in every one of my classes except Fine Arts. She exudes the confidence of a prepared person, someone who has done the work, read the assignments, listened to the teacher, asked questions, and conducted meaningful internal topical debate. Martha is short, strong, redheaded, and profoundly freckled. She has the unruffled ease of a surgeon as she goes about her essay, laying out two pencils beside her for backup.

The door behind me is open, an autumn morning breeze coming in and rustling our papers. Like the crackling hooks of Velcro, thoughts scatter in my mind, looping and getting snagged with my own undigested pain and discomfort of what I have yet to resolve in my own world.

The Romans were expansive conquerers and enslaved those they conquered.

American slavery was first British slavery, and then we just didn't stop it when we had the chance during the creation of the Constitution. How could we have missed that?

American slavery was an extension of the global trafficking of human beings, and it developed an industry considered essential to commerce in the rural South.

Are we learning as a race and becoming better or is George Orwell right in his portrayal of 1984 now just ten years away? Perhaps we are all still slaves to BIG BROTHER and just don't know it!

And the Romans are Catholic. Dear God, this is confusing.

Maybe this is why Dr. Worthin wants us to write about it, yet where to start? I begin with a mental map to distinguish two ways they are similar and two ways they are different to settle my morning mind: stomach growling audibly and boots tight around my right calf, which is slightly larger than the other. I tap into a well of insight and aggravation and begin: In the Roman Empire, slaves were often white, considered human, and could become free. The British Empire enslaved people of color—Africans and Indians—and built economies that required the exploitation . . . *Crack!* My pencil breaks not at the tip, but fully at the center, and my hand clutches the two pieces.

Martha, without missing a beat, takes one of her backup pencils and places it on my paper without my even asking or before I begin to look for another of my own. In a soft, inner smiling voice, she says to me without lifting her head from her work, "Damn Kentucky pencils." My heart lifts and I smile broadly and, without catching myself, laugh out loud, drawing in a breath and accidental attention. Martha and I catch eyes, and I send her my deep thanks. In this exact moment, I know that someone has heard me—my offhand, snarky comments about how bad Kentucky is, my loneliness, my pride about the forests and oceans of my homeland.

All in one act of natural service, Martha has let me know that she sees me, accepts me, and can make fun of my prejudices in a mere three words. That is marksmanship. We both know the pencil wood probably came from Washington. The moment marks a shift within me as a fourteen-year-old, as I become more aware of the impact of my thoughts and words. It will be many, many, *many* years, though, before I understand how deeply the righteous justification of hatred of those who hate runs, or how it is a part of my own legacy and that of the world I was incarnated into to serve.

When you look within,

*find where humor helps you lighten up to see the layers
of judgment and right-fighting opinions.*

Where have your words impacted the perspective of another's future? How is the handing down of beliefs shaping the world without your full permission? Are you blocking your ability to love and appreciate people because you are being loyal to an unexamined judgment of them? What if you instead love and appreciate them for the possibility they hold? How can you learn to love the haters without condoning the hatred? Instead of judgment, let curiosity and humor be your tour guides. Let a little lightness lift the layers to loosen the Velcro-tight grip of what *is* in exchange for what *could be*.

6

Choosing Choice

La Jolla, California

Snapshot One: The Pannikin Coffee Shop

April 1980

The Pannikin, with its outdoor tables under low-slung trees, as well as its strong coffee and space to spread books out to study, has become my place to study . . . a small slice of heaven. Taking the number thirty bus all the way back from my road-side cottage rental to the UCSD library takes too much time out of my day—or so I tell myself—although perhaps it is the wonder of a semi-European experience that my better-traveled friends have helped me envision that has made this local coffeehouse a home for my mind. For me, this is an era before time constraints become an ever-present force, before computers or the internet. I can easily work at the middle table under the big tree for hours without blinking—or spending more than $2.75.

Drafting a rough essay on a yellow legal pad, flipping back and forth, capturing references, and pausing to consider how to bring the mighty ideas of Buckminster Fuller and Marshall McLuhan together, I tap on my second-year calculus book with my left hand in hopes of spontaneous knowledge transmission via my fingertips.

I look up. A petite young man with dark curly hair and eyelashes that could shelter a family of four from a tropical rainstorm sits across from me.

At point-blank range, he asks, "What are you studying?"

My mind sputters out of library mode and this sheer mental "pull-up" from my focused concentration to the level of casual conversation startles me, and I speak before assembling socially graceful words.

"This." I spread my hands to indicate the whole of it; my current moment of the incongruity of math, futurism, and communications theory, wishing the books could and would express the integration of ideas that awaited me.

"I am Suranjith, yet call me Sunji, son of Valentine."

We proceed to speak for hours, about the celebrated anthropologist couple living on top of Mt. Soledad, just a mile up the hill where the million-dollar views are, and where Sunji is a house guest who brings to academic study the beyond-Linda-Blair-type exorcism practices of Sri Lankan Catholic branches. We talk about the Himalayas, German ex-pats living in Bombay, the weather in London, cricket, rugby, his father Valentine's remarkable architecture for the disadvantaged and for the sacred, and Sunji's so many brothers with such long names! All things new to me—the rushing, joyful stimulation of greeting stories from another world.

We talk until sunset.

I walk home alone, along Pearl Street, stepping back into my academic life from an exotic, mind-stretching trip across planet Earth to the Himalayas, back through the familiar threshold of the side door of my cottage and into the kitchen.

La Jolla, California

Snapshot Two: The Pannikin Coffee Shop
April 1980: The Very Next Day

Again sitting at the middle table under the tree, the place that positive habit had conditioned me to gravitate to and that had yielded many fine study sessions, I spread my feast of books and note pads, and hold my ceramic coffee mug like a Nordic scepter, invoking the gods of reason to visit sooner rather than later. Now with a strong idea under partial construction, its pieces falling into place, at least enough for today—with formulas revealing sequence and rhythm as I work through the less familiar territory of integral mathematics—I stand, stretching, and refill my scepter for fifty cents at the counter, adding at least twenty cents of half-and-half. *Thank you, Pannikin!*

Making my way back from the counter and down the steps to the patio, I return to my table and there he is. Sitting and smiling.

Waiting. For me.

I return the smile, partially startled and partially embarrassed by my messy table.

"How are you today, Suuuzee?" he continues without waiting for my response. "I see you are a busy, busy gull." A subtle shift in my brain lets me know he has said "girl," not "gull," yet I love that he says "girl" this way. "Look at all these books, and here you are again today! Did you sleep well? Have you been thinking about me? Of course you have. I have been thinking about you . . ." A stream of semi-conscious questions arises from him as I turn inward and ask myself, *Have I been thinking of him? No. Should I have been thinking of him? Maybe? Now I am thinking about whether I ought to be thinking about him. What does that mean?*

My mind drifts to my freshman professor of Greek philosophy and the intricacies of enlightenment through inquiry, yet I feel the early pull of a loop—a mind loop. The Susanne of today would be able to see that a mind-looping question has been ever so subtly set. The Susanne of this snapshot is in the early stages of a condition that would take me decades to unwind. A mind-looping question has no valuable answer. It wastes and redirects the energy of the mind by creating more questions, essentially leading to doubt, guilt, exhaustion, or all of the above.

Guilt, which I have allowed Sunji to give me, operates with greater ground cover than doubt. Its brew of urgency and obligation is likely to generate regrettable actions from an incorrect place. Doubt is likely to block correct actions. We know what to do, yet we do not do it. Guilt becomes the inner judge (I am guilty), jury (self-condemnation), and executioner (punishment and death). Guilt and doubt are collaborating cousins, *and* they are consumers of energy, not generators, thus leaving us depleted.

Unaware that I have been derailed, my undisciplined nineteen-year-old mind has a tinge of *I have done something wrong by not thinking about this man that I had an interesting conversation with yesterday. He has just arrived in this country, and I suppose it's my job to be welcoming . . . oh, and perhaps there is something I ought to be doing for him. I mean, he* has *been thinking about me* . . . The train of my being is now leaving the station of my own soul for parts unknown.

Yes, it happens *that* fast. And that benignly!

I ease into my seat at the table, my coffee in hand and eyes down, brushing imaginary crumbs off my lap habitually, stumbling into the awareness that I am wearing fuchsia lot-dyed painter pants from my summer of 1979 New York City visit. Pants so bright they can probably be seen from space.

He continues. "I'm fine, how are yooouuu?" Directing emphasis on the "yooouuu" relieves the unrecognized pressure and releases my let's-call-it-guilt for not thinking about him. Of course, I fail to see that this mindset of guilt has already been inserted, that I have now allowed it in, and that I am a resourceful, ready subject.

I fail to see that I have failed to see.

Awash with enthusiasm, sharing all his ideas from a twilight inspiration, Sunji continues without missing a step. "I've been telling you, Suuuzie, darling, how I am. Are you listening?" His imploring eyes and forehead lean over my books.

"We must go to Goa . . . no, to Dharamsala . . . no, to Pakistan! I could dress you as a man. Can you get your hair all up in a knot under a helmet? Are you good on a bike? A motorbike. We need to buy a motorbike . . . at least a 250cc . . . that will work." He inhales as punctuation. "Yes, it is time to return to India and get out of this country," he muses, unaffected by my silence, as if we had talked the whole idea through and speaking to me as if from a thousand years of knowing one another.

I am silent, computing the incongruity of his urgency, thinking to myself, "Hey, you just got here, dude, so what is the rush?" The knowing of our future is seemingly on his side rather than mine, as his stream of ideas shakes me awake and asleep at the same time. I can say now the rush was part of his "rush," the cortisol of chaos, which I mistook for adventure.

How am I now, "darling"? I wonder.

The stream continues. "You must go . . . you must go with me. I can show you. I dreamt it."

The uttering of possibility and reality in such rapid fire makes the books on the table begin to feel small in comparison to the door opening right in front of me.

Make no mistake: I find Sunji quite attractive, yet in an intellectual way, not as a boyfriend or lover. His enthusiasm and perspective on life are unmatched by anyone I have met (granted, I am only nineteen). Talking with him on this spring day, the idea of going to India is very appealing.

We leave the cafe together, books and partially written paper returned to my backpack, to walk the La Jolla Cove, its Dr. Seuss trees of all shapes silhouetted against the beauty of the sea.

As we begin to walk back up the hill, he touches me on my right butt cheek, and I recoil with an internal violence that I do not verbalize. *Is this normal? Why did he do that? I do not like that. I want nothing to do with him.* I override my instincts and keep walking, politely listening.

My body tells me "no," but my obligation and sense of being a good person muffle that message of wisdom into obscurity. How many ways would my life be different had I, in that very moment, been able to bring to language and say what I felt in a way that could be heard? I missed my point of choice by remaining silent.

Take Two: Susanne Conrad, April 1980, La Jolla Cove Park. "Hey, Sunji, I don't want to be touched like that. I *do* enjoy talking with you and learning from you. I would enjoy being your friend if you believe you can work with those boundaries. I do not want to be your girlfriend, or lover."

Yet I do not say any of this, and later in the relationship, when I do, Sunji does not believe my "no." He will chuckle and quote Gertrude from *Hamlet*: "The lady doth protest too much, methinks."

I learn how to smother my own "no," and in doing so, muddle the waters of choice. The Line of Choice goes missing. I cannot cross over what I cannot see. I am lost, yet still so bright, so happy, so alive, so willing.

Rudderless in wide waters.

. . .

Del Mar, California
July 29, 1981
1:30 a.m.

I enter the living room from the kitchen and see a halo of blue light from the television shining through carefully permed, fine hair. Placing a TV tray featuring my best orchestration of tea and cakes in front of the chair, anticipation sparkles from my ninety-four-year-old housemate, the static electricity of fantasy intersecting with reality. I hustle to keep up.

It is o-dark-thirty in the morning, and my client, my indirect employer, my housemate, and my responsibility, Mrs. Helen Moss of Del Mar, California, and I are up to watch the live, televised broadcast of the marriage of Diana Frances Spencer to Charles, Prince of Wales. I brew a small pot of tea for myself also to stay awake, as the event is not nearly as relevant to me as it is to Mrs. Moss. She encourages me to call her Helen, but because I am just twelve days past the legal drinking age, it only seems proper to call her Mrs. Moss.

I have been living with her as her sole caretaker while continuing my full-time course load at UCSD now for over six months. Naturally, we are growing close. I learn that Mrs. Moss married a mining engineer and lived in many places, including Venezuela, where she tamed a wild bobcat who became her companion. I know she never had children, yet I've never learned why. I *have* learned how to make ice cream out of avocados, lemon, and sugar, though. Jim, my predecessor in this role, taught me all the different things that Mrs. Moss likes: the apportioned breakfasts before leaving the two-bedroom duplex for morning classes, the meticulous raspberry jam and cream cheese sandwiches on Pepperidge Farm thin-sliced white bread sealed in square Tupperware containers for freshness and easy autonomous retrieval at lunch while I am away, and the delicate dishes I prepare for dinner, which generally include sauces and always a glass of sherry in a petite cut-crystal micro goblet. My duties include meal preparation, washing dishes and clothing, shopping, cleaning of the nighttime commode, personal bathing, and help with dressing, although Mrs. Moss has that one dialed in with her fanciful collection of front-zippered housecoats that rotate through our days together.

This morning's early rise of tea-making and wedding-watching is a once-in-a-lifetime duty of pleasure.

"Look at that!" Mrs. Moss exclaims, pointing a frail yet intentional right index finger at the television set as we glimpse Diana veiled next to her father in a classic, Cinderella-style, horse-drawn carriage. Crowds along the street cheer loudly, steady like the roar of a surging sea, as the carriage rides an enormous unseen wave of adoration. Diana emerges as the commentator trills about the dress, its length, origin, making, materials—the extravagant gown simultaneously overpowers and amplifies the soul within it.

"That is amazing!" I share with gusto. "More keeps coming out! How much fabric is in there?" We both chortle, transfixed to the screen.

The pageantry continues. Mrs. Moss is settled in her nest of granny-square afghan contentment, mouth wide and open in gawking awe, the downy, baby-bird-like fuzz on her head blowing in the fanned night air. She has often shared with me how her family would take horse-drawn carriages from San Diego to La Jolla to stay at the beach as an ocean holiday. Her father transported their family from the East to the West very early after the transcontinental railway was completed, relocating for health reasons, as was often the case in those days—changing the whole of an environment without, to cure what was within. Mrs. Moss lived to see the transformation from horse-drawn carriages to transcontinental trains, to automobiles to airplanes, missiles, and moon landings.

I retreat to my own bedroom to rest for a while before the sun is up and it will be time again to study. I stretch out on my unmade bed in the pre-dawn. My two open, double-hung windows face west and I hear the night ocean, the sound lifting from the sand, up the cliffs, over the train tracks to my left ear, as my right ear processes the sounds seeping through the wall from the royal wedding, such as the changing of the guard of the TV tray, making way for access to her walker. I hear Mrs. Moss rise steadily from her chair, the rhythmic sound of her efforts echoing across the living room as she makes her way to the bathroom and back again safely. Offering the grace of non-interference, staying quiet in my room, I recognize her eighteen-minute round-trip as an expression of independence and choice.

The summer air that wafts in is wet with the marine layer that places droplets of condensation democratically on all things—bougainvillea, hibiscuses, and sandy flip-flops, once dried, but now wet again. The tide makes the sand smooth and new again with each pull of the moon, leaving a renewal of nutrients and a caressing forgiveness of the previous twelve hours of activity. Tracks of both sand crab and sandcastles are erased, replaced with the withdrawing sea's artistry.

Placing my hands on my chest, I attempt to sing myself to sleep:
"Every day, oh every way,
I feel I'm growing, day by day,
Every day, in every way,
I feel I'm growing."

I made up this song for myself shortly after returning from India with Sunji last summer. I sing it aloud when appropriate, and within as needed while pumping up the hills on my bike with an old canvas newspaper bag across my shoulders brimming with laundry, listing to the right to balance the bag on my left, my pockets weighted with quarters.

I've stopped giving myself permission to pity myself in any dimension since returning from India and Sri Lanka. I've traveled to Mexico and Canada, but not anywhere at all like India, where the smells and sounds of birth and death collide, and in my case, overwhelm, like a gong of experiences in the library of my mind, yet no ready file folders exist for what I have seen and smelled. A stack of unresolved cases sits on the desk of my heart. When I left India, I promised myself I would not return until I had something to give. A sense of powerless privilege weighed on my young shoulders, and I tucked the intention to create a form of universal empowerment into a crack in my broken heart.

I had my twentieth birthday in Dharamsala, awaiting a glimpse of the Dalai Lama in his home after escaping from China. I did not see him, yet I met the Tibetan people that lived there and had traveled en masse with him out of China. I ate marvelous noodles after what felt like ages of rice and heat in the south and received the high mountain rain and green steamed vegetables with gratitude.

There are many stories from Sri Lanka and Southern and Northern India, yet I hold within me confusion and condemnation, transformation and wonder.

Allow me to digress. No, I mean truly and fully digress. Stay with me.

Sunji and I returned from India late in the summer of 1980 and spent a few days with our friend Jim in Del Mar while we found a place to live. Already, I was having natural feelings such as "we" would find a place to live. There had been no conversation of consequence about who would pay and who would decide. There was a given, an unspoken, never-negotiated reality that I would pay and Sunji would decide. How did this situation happen to the "Striking Viking," as my college counselors wrote of me in letters of reference, a summa cum laude graduate of the Kentucky Country Day School and now about to enter my third year of university with a similarly impressive academic record? How does a streaking comet of exuberance and intelligence, a daughter of progressive parents, submit personal power so readily to a stranger and become whatever I am in the process of becoming?

That is exactly the question I do not see, and thereby cannot ask.

The question then becomes, what blocks the seeing? In looking now, I can recognize that Suranjith knew who I was before I did. I do not see my kindness, intelligence, or power. My lack of self-awareness leaves me vulnerable—in the full sense of the word—open to attack, hurt, or wound as by a weapon. I have many "holes in my pocket," so to speak, so that others can tell me how I am, and I will believe them without testing their assertions myself. Perhaps this is why I have dedicated my life to the teaching of self-awareness as the source of leadership.

• • •

Del Mar, California
July 29, 1981
6:45ish a.m.

Mrs. Moss sleeps in past her normal rising time. Our night of partying with Diana and Charles has taken its toll on our routine. Rolling out of bed, I shuffle into the bathroom and start the hot water for my shower, circle through her room to see her resting deeply, and clean the night commode for the day ahead. Flushing the stale urine and rinsing the catching basin, I return it catlike to its resting place near her bed. A quick turn out her door into the micro hallway of a 1920s duplex, and I'm back in the bathroom.

Stepping into the stall and around the bathing chair, the water spreading from the crown of my head over my face, neck, and back, I instantly succumb to warmth and the private worlds of possibility that showers offer.

Shampooing my hair with Clairol Herbal Essence shampoo and conditioner, the scent transports me to middle school during the early 1970s and the whole-body sensation of financial well-being and safety that comes with using shampoo that your mom has paid for. At age twenty, I feel the impact of buying my own everything and that, of course, makes sense and is culturally responsible.

My parents have been unwilling to continue funding the cottage that Sunji and I rented in August 1980 after returning from India, for the many reasons that by now I have become blind to, and their withdrawal of support has led to me finding this caregiver role and housing with Mrs. Moss. Enjoying my small yet well-located room near the Pacific Ocean and North County bus line, I frugally use the $700 monthly salary from the State of California—my actual employer—to purchase Herbal Essence, fresh-ground peanut butter, and apples. All anyone my age really needs.

Turning and bending to my right, grabbing the soap bar from the inset, I rise through the steam and see a long hair stuck to the tile in an elegant shape.

I am stopped by its beauty and perfection.

Lifting my left arm to soap up, I turn to look again.

And then *I see.*

I know. Knowing like a thousand books uploading to my mind.

I choose.

Yes, it happens *that* fast.

Knowing what resides within and without as surely as the blood flows in my veins and the steamy air fills my lungs. I know that I know that I know. I did not know, until this very moment, that I *could* know, that I know that I know. My own long, dark blonde hair clinging to the mint green tiles speaks directly to me in the language of symbolism, of intuition—a language beyond language, yet foundational to all worlds and all futures. In the strand, I see the gestalt simple image of a veiled woman cradling a child—a hieroglyph of the heart, speaking the voices of ten thousand generations mothering humanity.

I know I am pregnant . . . a second time.

Months earlier, while living in the Del Mar rental cottage, I rode the bus up to the student medical center on an ordinary Thursday, after "dating" Sunji six months, after my last final of the academic trimester, with no one at my side—friend, lover, parent, or counselor. I lay down with an IV of Valium and had a perfectly legal, medically safe and sanctioned, $10 student co-pay abortion. I rode the bus home after resting an hour in the burnt-orange waiting room to make a dinner of brown rice and tofu stir-fry for a waiting group of friends celebrating the end of the school term. I was grateful for the simplicity. I told no one. Not even Sunji.

Here in the shower, I resolve again to tell no one. At least not until it is too late and too obvious, when time can protect me from the social outrage and uncertainty I will ultimately face. Time to protect me from Sunji's upset, to protect me from the convincing encouragement from others to not have the baby. The time to get to month four, when a simple $10 procedure will not be so simple. What has changed? I simply know. I listen to this deep-body-knowing strand of hair talking to me. I can still see it after all these years. I can draw it. It draws me in. I am both the mother and the mothered.

La coeur—"the heart" in French—is the root word for "courage." The guilt I feel about my guilt for not walking away from the knowing and disturbing touch on Day Two at the Pannikin, where I override my "no" for not "no"ing who I was and for getting lost and disconnected from my own, as-of-yet-unarticulated higher purpose, is strong. The downward spiral I travel, feeling guilt for feeling guilt, becomes something else. An outstretched hand of help adjusts the pulse and timing of this moment in the shower and steers me up and away from self-brutality by the grace and help of a single, not-so-stray hair.

I choose life and life chooses me simultaneously like two magnets connecting—neither myself nor life taking credit separately—a nanosecond of non-duality. The feeling of being *in* choice versus making *a* choice.

> *Choice becomes a space to join, to inhabit, to exist in fully and unapologetically. A place of origin and ultimate creativity. A loving, living NOW.*

Looking in the mirror and seeing oneself, free of the past, sensing the kindness and goodness of one's own two hands. This is the feeling of being *in* choice.

Confusion and condemnation resolve as transformation and wonder release cellularly. I step out of the shower a mother, knowing I am protected and guided by ten thousand generations. I step out knowing I am willing to protect and guide the next ten thousand to come. Amazing what a great shower can do.

7

Please, Stop Pleasing

Del Mar, California
October 1981

I know I need to let my parents know, but knowing they need to know doesn't help me. The knowing-something part of me and doing-something part of me are not talking. They are not collaborating, integrating, or creating. These parts know this, yet they aren't doing anything about it. They watch and wait while judging and protecting their positions.

Pregnancy is at once the most personal of states and public of outcomes, becoming quite visible even when you are young, fit, and 5' 10"—with lots of torso space to hide a baby. My parents are at the height of enjoying world travel, being empty nesters, and buying new cars. My father is now five years post intestinal bypass surgery and has a completely new life, wardrobe, and sense of identity. They live 3,000 miles away and are just turning fifty, so are still quite young. They have not dreamed of being grandparents, and the pangs of "I wish you two would settle down and have a family" are not part of the dialogue.

"Communicate, goddammit."

"No management through surprise."

Clearly, I am in violation of several of my father's prime and sub-prime directives. They echo in my mind and violently argue with my knowing-part and doing-part. Nothing. More sitting. Sadness. I am reading *Magical Child* by Joseph Chilton Pearce, learning how important the emotional mindset of the mother is for the development of the unborn child. How do I shift myself from celebrating my choice to facing Suranjith, and my father's anger and disappointment, which is likely around the corner? Of course, I have no true idea of my parents' reactions, yet they are already happening in my mind. Whole imaginary conversations take place. Sitting cross-legged on my bed in Mrs. Moss's home, I lean against the pillows and the wall. I replay on a loop the conversation I had yesterday with Sunji:

"What?" screamed Sunji.

"Yes, I just found out."

"What the hell?" He clutches the keys to the motorcycle and mimes throwing them in my face from ten inches away.

Silence. I do not flinch, as I am not looking at him, rather down at my encroaching and unkept cuticles.

"How could you do this?"

I turn my left index finger inward and push back the skin with my right index finger to reveal the half moon.

"You're fucking up my plans, man."

I look up.

He knows he has my attention. "What are you going to do?"

I click into "neck-up mode" and dully respond, being intentionally and righteously practical. "I am going to work, go to school, and have a baby."

"Suzy, you're fucking up my life."

Some deep Catholic or Hindu value of life and family begins to emerge out of this raging fire and his tone changes: "Well, he'll be a sweet boy, I know." His voice softening, his inner eyes looking to a new horizon.

"We don't know if the baby will be a boy or a girl." My jab of being right and rational.

"He is a boy."

Silence on my end.

"He will love his sweet daddy."

"Yes, I am sure."

A brief silence.

"You're fucking up my plans!"

In my family, great value is placed on communication, yet not authentic conversation. Growing up, communication was more like reporting or broadcasting, which was indeed a giant step up from keeping secrets, as was the case with other families I knew while going to high school in Louisville.

"Gosh, Carol, your mom's not around much today. How is she?" I had once asked my good friend when we were sophomores.

"Oh, she's here," Carol said.

"Where?" I said, looking around the vast walnut cabinet kitchen with servant sub-kitchen through the short hall, used when Carol's mom hosted large parties.

"She's sleeping."

"At lunchtime?"

"Yeah, she sleeps a lot. She's not well."

Carol's mom was an alcoholic.

So the report and broadcast communication strategy of the world of the Gablins seems a world of enlightenment beyond secret-keeping.

Do I call my parents on a Saturday morning? They are three hours ahead of me, now living in Washington, D.C., where Dad is consulting and lobbying and Mom is reporting, researching, and authoring a scientific newsletter called *Radwaste News* that keeps the industry abreast of new legislation governing the civilian and military worlds of radioactive waste.

I imagine and internally run through the scenario that will play out.

"Hi, Mom. Hi, Dad."

"Hi, sweetie, how are you?" Mom will say on one phone extension. "How are your classes?"

Dad will overlay on the other extension before I can answer Mom.

"Oh, I like Population Ecology. I'm learning to code and programming a model of island ecosystems." I will offer this information to delight and distract Dad.

"Oh you know, honey," he will say, "Admiral Grace Hopper invented COBOL. She's one of the first women to reach her rank and her research . . ."

Then Dad will go on for eleven minutes or more, branching related tangents about the evolution of computer code and the navy, and women in the service, and who he has met, and what I ought to be thinking about for my career, because of course, I would make a great scientist, and General Atomic is right here in the San Diego area, and I will wait for a moment to interject, perhaps even interrupt . . . maybe when he starts to talk about a guy he met over a Heineken that—

"Hey, Mom and Dad, I have news. I'm pregnant!" I will say this with positive inflection, the way I would speak to calm my father out of a brewing rage towards me or my mother or my goddammed choices and to stop him from uttering, "What the hell? Your brain has gone to mush in California and the taxes are ridiculous and fruitcakes live out there and goddammit, is that little creep the father? I won't have this. You are fucking up my life!"

I will continue with rational conviction and say, "Hey, I weighed the options and built a decision matrix and held a board meeting presenting my life plan to world authorities and they agreed that after my previous $10 Valium abortion, and even with the undiscovered risks of sharing a child with a narcissistic, spiritually abusive lost soul, and after the loss of my personal dignity, and an extension on my higher education for at least two years, it will all turn out all right, and ultimately I will be the source of a catalytic and universal system of self-leadership that will help hundreds of thousands of people step out of fear and doubt and into the light of their own beauty. So I've said yes to it all, you see, and I thought you two would love to be part of the adventure, although the Board told me there would be a catch and that I will forget and be confused and sometimes ridiculed, and that you will oscillate between being upset and delighted, but that in the end you will be very proud and happy even though you will sometimes argue privately about whose fault it is that I got pregnant in a world of birth control pills and the full-on sexual revolution. *So* I said yes, I understand, and I checked the box on the universal agreement and terms and conditions, and the Board said yes to my yes and let me know. Oh, and did I tell you that all of this happened when I looked at one of my own hairs stuck to Mrs. Moss's shower tile?"

I will say all of this and they will understand, and there will be nothing to defend or prove or convince or justify. We will be on the phone in total understanding of all the choices, all the glory, all the joy before us, and we will celebrate the miracle of this perfect child, this future world champion, this baby held in waiting, patient love from all sides, all dimensions, all realities. And we will smile at our glorious future together.

I decide to write a notecard instead.

I choose the Impressionist Monet and his water-lily work for $1.49. I buy the card at the Del Mar bookstore down the street from the place where my dad likes to get coffee and a danish when he visits. I write the basics and trust Monet to help me, so that when my parents yell, they yell at each other and not me. I cannot take any more. I have no place for it. No shield, no deflection, no protection. My heart opened wide with oxytocin and my "yes," and God knows what other hormones are already changing my world and building a liver, and a heart, and a mini-everything miraculously out of peanut butter, apples, and carrot juice from Windmill Farms.

On the fourth day, the telephone rings. This is a telephone, not a cell phone. It has physical attachments to the wall and the world through a vast wiring system, tunneling through mountains, cabled under oceans arising to each home. Mrs. Moss inhabits her post in her living room with the command force of a decorated five-star general. A tapestry wingback chair with a specialized pillow supports her back and regal posture, and she directs her life with purpose. From this post, Helen can see the front door, the television, into the small hallway, into my room when the door is open, out the front windows, and she can hear all the goings-on in the kitchen. Navy SEALs would envy Helen's placement, as she is both undercover and has direct visual access through most of her home as well as the street outside.

On her side table lie a book, glasses, teacup, and a mini spiral notebook with a pen and rubber band, which holds pieces of paper in place with handwritten addresses, people of measure, and telephone numbers since 1928; also arrayed are random photos, breath mints, a silver hairbrush, and most importantly, the telephone. Her command-center dashboard. Her walker, placed slightly in front of her, gives space for her to cross her ankles unimpeded. Black-and-white photo albums are stacked within reach on a lower shelf beneath the surface of the turned-dowel-legged table, the images a historical account of her days in Venezuela. Here she can be seen stroking her pet bobcat as she gazes at a mountain range, and the long thick skirt, though still in this picture, can be imagined as blowing in the wind. Captured in time in these photographs is her small waist, and the very same eyes.

Brrrring. The telephone on the loudest setting blares into my ears, and before the end of the second ring, Helen has nabbed the handset.

"Hello, Helen here," she answers with the precision of a telephone operator and the expectancy of a child at Christmas. "Yes, yes, Susanne is here (1001, 1002, 1003) . . . yes, yes, I am doing well . . . she is a better cook than Jim was, you know (1004, 1005, 1006) . . . yes, yes, I will get her."

Without a doubt, the callers are my parents. I walk from my room, smile at Helen with tragic sensations in my stomach, and fetch the extra cord wound up between the wall and her side table, the dust bunnies hopping up into the air between us. Everything is between everything, and she says, "Here she is!" as she extends her reach to hand me the whole of the telephone.

"Hi, Mom . . . hang on just a sec," I mutter, then hold the receiver against my chest and retreat cautiously to my bedroom and mostly close the door with the cord running through the crack.

Here I would like to write fabulous dialogue that captivates you and takes you to the edge of your seat—*And what next?* you'd wonder—and I would hold your hand with my words and together bring us to a loving insight about moments in life that matter. You would marvel at the precision of my memory to recount the conversation with my mother and father, and it would rekindle in you a charged memory, and later, you would handwrite a letter to me on a smaller than normal-sized card about the time you shared with your parents a difficult reality—that your brother, their son, overdosed somewhere in Indonesia and "Yes, we need to meet the body at LAX"—or that you performed infant CPR on your baby that died in her sleep and could I understand, *please,* because you *need* someone to understand, or that you spent the night shaking off roofies and scrubbing out sperm from a stranger when you wished the friend with you could have helped you reel your soul back into your body and collect DNA evidence to give to the sex crimes unit in a mini-shampoo bottle from your workout bag because without it they said, "Sorry, we can't help you, Miss."

And I would write you back that day with the love and validation that can only come from outside one's family of origin. Not because anything is wrong with your family. Or maybe because everything is right with your family. But you don't trust them when they say, "You are smart and beautiful and wonderful." You disregard the praise as untrue and drift sideways into your own flawed self-view. Yet in the reading of this fabulous dialogue to come, and the beautiful note you receive from me in the mail, you would see all of that and liberate yourself from the lie. You would shed the unshed tears, the tears burning new eyes into being. You would meet me later at a workshop in Northern California or, better yet, in Fiji, because neither of us have been and we hear it is a nice place, and we find each other and hug and laugh at the miracle of our connection.

Yet I am not able to write that fabulous dialogue.

Leaning against the wrought-iron headboard, pillows piled up against it to soften the bars rigid against my spine, I sit cross-legged, placing the base of the telephone on the white chenille bedspread.

Sunji is in my room, squatting, back against the wall, as there is no chair. We look at each other and he watches me prepare to speak. I am accustomed now to his frequent visits. His front door into my life is the set of double-hung bedroom windows. He goes around to the backyard, where an orange crate is the step stool, and climbs in. It is outside in the narrow back walkway behind my bedroom window that Sunji has commandeered as his hangout spot to smoke his unique, hand-crafted combination of tobacco and hash in an Indian pottery pipe called a "chillum." Other people gather there when they want to smoke with Sunji or when they want to visit me and do not want to bother with the formalities of small talk with Mrs. Moss. This is the same window that, a few weeks ago, I leaned out to smell the ocean and saw my friend Veronica had come. We talked and I told her my news and she said, "Oh, how fun! Let's have a baby!" And we laughed and I felt the warm sun of one person speaking in agreement with my future and meeting me there in happiness.

Sunji looks up at me, knowing this is "The Call."

"We got your letter," Dad says. I listen clearly, knowing I have decidedly "managed by surprise," thereby violating Gablin family protocol. He continues in a curious direction, asking, "Can you be friends with him?"

Without taking the time to breathe or consider the question or the intention, I muster the calm intelligent Susanne that has answers. "Sure," I say, nodding at Sunji with his elbows on his knees, watching like a cat. "I can be his friend."

Then, like a commanding bolt of unquestionable logic, Dad says—with Mom still quiet on the phone—"You are going to get married. I don't want to be a grandfather, no less the grandfather of a bastard."

No preamble, no "How are you feeling?"

No "Are you okay?"

It is about him and his social status, and yes, I know that, and no, I don't understand the impact of that on my life, and yes, I am not okay, and no, I don't know how to say that without being asked, and no, I don't know how to ask myself that.

To be fair to my dad, in retrospect, this is what I recall him saying. He may have said many other wonderful and emotionally congruent things that I was unable to hear.

"Okay," I say, faster than comprehension. *Okay* to get off the phone, *okay* to exit the discomfort, *okay* without meaning or understanding. *Okay?*

"Okay," I repeat. "Okay, we'll get married."

Sunji's eyes flare up at me, and he rises from his place against the wall. To this day, I can tell you that marrying Sunji was not even an option I'd considered or spoken of or wanted in any way or fashion, and yet out of my mouth come the words "Okay, we'll get married."

The whole 100-car freight train of my future life swerves onto another track as this twenty-one-year-old, cross-legged and sitting on my bed, speaks a world into being all because I don't want to upset or disappoint my parents.

"I want to talk to Sunji," Dad says. "Is he there?"

I don't lie yet want to. "Yes, he's right here."

Sunji's face reddens underneath his brown skin and the veins in his neck enlarge. I move to hang my legs off the bed, and he sits beside me, taking the receiver into his hand. With bravado and his slight British-accented English, he says, "Good morning, Ken . . . Good morning, Trula."

I do not know what my parents then say to him.

I live the outcome.

The next day, October 7, 1981, we are married in the Vista County

Courthouse by a woman judge. That same evening, I drive Sunji from Del Mar to LAX, and he flies as planned to Sri Lanka.

The way the downward spiral works, though, is that when it is spiraling, we can feel incredibly out of control and unable to change course. Consider where in *your* life you are pleasing someone or some established social norm without voice or question. How could your life be different if you listened to your body, to its signals and instincts? Where are you saying "okay" when it or you is actually *not* "okay" at all?

Perhaps the greatest act of self-actualization
is to choose choice.

To find it in the dark, knowing it is always there for one who calls it into existence. I chose to write about this moment in my life to shine light on how the degrading orbit of self-brutality works and compounds, yet it can be interrupted and reversed at any time. Even after the fact. Especially after the fact. Question the fact. We have the choice to clear the trauma of the past without erasing the memory, and thereby bring personal power to bear in all arenas.

8

Release Your
Inherited Legacy

La Jolla, California
Fall 1981

The main library at UCSD is an architectural peculiarity—all concrete and glass rising out of a eucalyptus tree grove. Polarizing opinions about its looks make it a campus conversation piece. For me, the library is an interior experience, and with every visit I find a new corner and a new book. Even after all my years of visiting, the library turns a man-made thingness into nature, like the ocean offering up a bit of weathered brick so round I mistake it for a stone. A perpetual invitation for discovery.

The books are organized in sections by topics, allowing me to browse as I would in a bookstore without having to already know what book I am looking for. A book catches my eye at thigh height, and I pull it out. This one is longer than normal, more of a picture book format. I am attracted to its structure, perhaps from the classes with Phil Steinmetz, the photography professor that I am studying with. Phil learned his craft under Ansel Adams, being one of the young mentees carrying the large-format cameras into the mountains and canyons.

As I draw the book out, and read the title, *Immaculate Deception* by Suzanne Arms, I drop to the floor with it in my lap and begin to flip through its pages, stroking the fierce black-and-white photographs with my fingertips as if there is also Braille to inform me, conjuring images from the irony of her title.

. . .

The bus ride from Del Mar to downtown San Diego where the midwives have their office has one transfer and takes a giant bite out of my morning. I arrive hungry and late. Walking up two flights of stairs and into a space both warm and clinical, a bell jingles at my arrival. Family-style Polaroid photos are thumbtacked to a thin strip of corkboard wrapping around the receiving area at eye level. Babies and moms and dads and brothers and sisters and grandparents and neighbors and friends and more babies of all colors (partly because getting oneself born can turn a person red or purple) circle me. I sign in, not at a desk, but by simply putting my name on a clipboard on the coffee table next to "How To" books and stapled-together lists of baby names and their meanings.

There is an essay-style intake packet to fill out. I see a small, plexiglass tabletop sign in both English and Spanish that reads "Please Complete Our Receiving Packet. Thank you. The Midwives of San Diego." I can see that it is at least four pages in length, and I settle in for the duration. With a rumbling tummy, I look over and see a

Sparkletts water dispenser with funnel paper cups and a basket beside it filled with nuts, crackers, and granola bars. On the handle of the basket is a handwritten note, looped and stapled, declaring in practical empathy "Help Yourself . . . We Know," with a heart drawn as the period of the exclamation mark. Before I even meet any of the midwives, my body is eating and drinking in this place and these people. I begin my Receiving Packet.

There is the regular stuff such as address and phone number, yet very quickly, even before asking about health history, the packet takes a turn I have never considered. Instead of checking a box with "married" or "single," the form begins its open-ended mind blow:

Question One: Describe your current living situation.

Question Two: Why do you want to give birth at home with a midwife?

Question Three: Where do you see yourself giving birth?

Question Four: Who do you see being there?

Question Five: What questions, concerns, or fears do you have about giving birth? If this is your first child, how do you feel about becoming a parent? Please describe your support network.

Question Six: Do you have health insurance?

Question One rivets me to reality: I am a twenty-one-year-old full-time USCD student living in Del Mar as a caretaker of a ninety-four-year-old (primarily shut-in) woman. Then there is all that I *want* to write yet hesitate. I am under review on this first visit because I am coming to the clinic six months pregnant. I am legally married, yet in reality, I am a married single mother.

Question Two: The hospital looks deadly, archaic, and soulless.

Question Three: Dear God, I have no idea. Good question.

Question Four: Blank stare.

Question Five: Blank mind.

Question Six: No, not yet.

A spry, thirty-something woman with soft reddish hair spun up in a French twist with a wisp dancing over her forehead and freckles spread across her cheekbones welcomes me with eyes that lock on mine and then release. She moves down the hall, supporting the elbow of a *super*-pregnant woman who is holding the hand of a young boy. The three of them glide as one, feet barely lifting. The woman's shape stuns me. How could anyone be that pregnant? How can she still walk? Does it hurt? Will she be okay? They emerge into the reception place and converse quietly. The boy squats by the snack basket and looks up as the pregnant woman nods a gentle approval. They continue towards the exit and I see in my mind the flights of stairs ahead of them. *Amazing. Brave. Real. Whoa.*

The freckled woman sits across from me and tucks the wisp into the whole of her updo. Her eyes take me in like a scanner on *Star Trek*, kind and logical. Not like how men do. Not all men. Just the men that do. They start where they are most attracted, a pop of color or a pop of cleavage—a curve that addicts—and then their eyes scan up and down, heads tilting to avoid looking like a stare. It's not a stare, though, it's a scan. I have been scanned in this way, and I have watched men look at whole groups of women in megascan mode. I do not know what happens inside their minds or even if what I am writing is true. It is my experience. The meaning I add without questioning.

After we remodeled our Vashon home, and Dory and I each had our own bedrooms, the large, modern bookcase system that came from an office furniture sale somewhere became the storage spot for my father's collection of *Playboy* magazines. I traveled my inner adolescent journey with the companionship of foldouts of naked, preened women from the 1960s for comparison.

I watch the freckled woman look at me.

She begins with my feet, sensing up my legs, then torso, and meets my eyes directly. "You must be Susanne, then," she states with matter-of-fact warmth.

"Yes." I'm feeling forthright now and grateful to be talking to a person instead of attempting to write open-ended essay questions with no preparation.

"It looks like you have begun filling in your packet. Let's do the rest together as a way to get to know each other."

I feel both the relief of a professor saying, "I'll help you with the in-class quiz" and the stress of a professor saying, "I'll help you with the in-class quiz." The relief of guidance and the stress of vulnerability. I am trained to be a prepared person with answers. Number One in the speed multiplication quizzes of third grade with Mrs. Stone. Once, Mrs. Stone took me out of class to ask me why I smirked when she asked the class to do an assignment. I do not know. I did not know I smirked.

It took me years to understand that, in third grade, I was bored. I did not know what bored was to tell Mrs. Stone. I only knew she did not like whatever she thought I did, and I felt ashamed, yet did not know what to be ashamed of. I did not know at that time what fragmentation felt like, as I did not yet have that name for it. Fragmentation comes from listening to the many unintegrated voices in our heads as if they matter, and especially as if they are telling us the truth.

One says: "I don't feel good."

The next one questions: "I didn't do anything wrong, so why do I feel bad?"

The next one says: "I don't know."

The next one answers: "I must, *must* BE wrong."

To make sense of this inner chaos, we break apart our wholeness and begin to pick on ourselves. It is a generally brutal civil war.

I have the picture of what married life looks like from my parents.

*I know what it feels like to say yes when I could have said
no, yet I do not know yet that what I need is no.*

I do not know yet what it feels like to be "out of choice"—the familiar, yet murky flow of doing what is expected.

This is what we called "inherited legacy" in Lightyear—the whole sea of unexamined patterns, beliefs, and biases that we are born into. This sea shapes and colors our thoughts and behaviors, often without our awareness. It is, as some say, "the sea we swim in," yet the fish asks, "What sea?"

Even today, as a sixty-year-old woman, I can tap into it: I am told "what you need to do, Susanne, is write a best-seller. Do a TED talk. Become famous. Gets lots of Instagram followers and then you will make a difference." How is that any different from "get an education, get married, have children, build a career or stay home, raise a few pets, visit family"? And then what? Where is the true star to steer from in any generation? I did not then know about the lower self. The splitting of my mind.

The lower self that just wants what it wants, and in particular, it wants continuity, mediocrity, and the "easy road." The continual tug between the social norm "shoulds" and the blue sky of possibility is beginning to divide my already-stressed self into two camps, perpetuating the drama of the civil war within.

Alone, lost on a chair in a room in downtown San Diego, a baby stirring in my belly, "I've got to get back to Mrs. Moss's by dinner" rattling in my mind, wondering about the bus schedule, I stop and say to the freckled woman, "Yes, I'd like that. I have a lot of questions and I know you have a lot for me."

"My name is Celia, and I'm a midwife. That means I deliver babies at home. I am not allowed to deliver babies in a hospital. If you need transport to a hospital for any reason, I will not be able to continue to care for you. I work with my partner, Ally, who is also a midwife. We have assistants that train with us. We need to ask you all these questions to help us create a picture of success. If you want a successful home birth, we are the people to work with."

Her directness of body and word slays my pretense and hesitation in one move. Sharing all of my life, perhaps for the first time to anyone, seems possible. The professors know my academic results but nothing of my personal situation; my parents love me yet want things different; Mrs. Moss I keep in the dark about the pregnancy and the window-crawling visits. Sunji is across the world, on one of his extended "business" trips in the "import-export" world. Many of the people around me have withdrawn now that Sunji is in India. Being accidentally coupled with a hashish addict (although in the moment I do not see him as that) has created a certain kind of social group with people who want to be high and people who want to be fed—fed on many levels.

Living at Mrs. Moss's has helped me be able to care for myself, though it is not the normal college living experience. I meet the occasional person in class and study with them, yet by late afternoon, I need to be off campus, back in Del Mar, setting up Mrs. Moss's TV tray and mini goblet of sherry. No dinners out. Sometimes a burrito from Roberto's Tacos. I do not feel sorry for myself. There is not time to cry, or rest, or reflect, or go to therapy, for God's sake—or even consider meeting another boy. I am locked down onto a train track of mother in reality and wife in imaginary. The purpose of being pregnant lifts the heavy fog daily. With all the books I have read, after my visit to Dharamsala, no one has seen me as Celia does.

Reading glasses slide down her slender nose and her middle finger adjusts them. Celia glances at my packet, smiling. "Let's begin at the beginning. Tell me about yourself, and where you live, what you do . . . a bit about your home life . . . that kind of thing."

"How much do you want to know?"

"As much as you want to tell. The more the better. Being a midwife is like being a lawyer. You want your midwife to know everything about your situation, because she is there to protect life, choice, and the human experience of birth. For a lawyer to be successful, they need to know their client's full situation."

Celia is not new to this and speaks with the calm inner authority of a woman who is practiced at being present; she does not skip steps with assumptions.

"My name is Susanne with an *s*. I am a full-time communications and public health student at UCSD. I am also a live-in caretaker for a ninety-four-year-old woman, Mrs. Moss, in Del Mar."

In what feels like a pause, I blurt out, "We live up on the cliffs and I take the bus to school." That is my way of saying, "I do not have a car."

"I took the bus here" is my way of saying, "I am tired, and I am far from home" without saying it.

"I've figured out how to do all my classes *and* have time to take care of Mrs. Moss. I read a book called *Immaculate Deception* and one called *Magical Child.* I am studying home birth on my own and found you by asking around. I don't know anyone who is pregnant, and you were very hard to find, but I figured there had to be midwives somewhere." That is my way of saying without saying, "See? I am diligent and disciplined and smart and please help me because I don't know how to ask for help."

"Well, you don't need to give birth at Mrs. Moss's house to have a home birth," Celia says with optimistic logic.

Her words are a rush of wind blowing into my mind—opening cellular windows of choices. Shutters clatter, their resistance to fresh perspectives giving way. The sensation of newness fills in the slivers, the cracks where my brain is wearing thin trying to "figure out" my future. It can be as simple as giving birth at someone else's house, yet I still need to sort out who will take over caring for Mrs. Moss. *Oh, and how will I make money?* Yet the wind keeps blowing and my mind calms and clears. Celia sits across from me and I wonder if she can see from my face that her comment has already altered my internal chemistry.

"I want to find the perfect place. I *can* find the perfect place. I can do that," I say to myself more than to Celia, and we move on in the spiraling way that conversations do, to what interests me about midwifery and home birth.

"In my history classes, I got to learn about the 'Bella Donnas,' the midwives, the herbalists, the witches of the Middle Ages and how they were systematically purged by the Catholic Church during the Inquisition. I have been putting that together with things I have been learning from *Diet for a Small Planet* and *Our Bodies, Ourselves* and Shakti Gawain's book on visualizing, and I read about the early cord-cutting and silver drops and the circumcisions the hospitals don't ask about before doing, and that seems wrong, and why wouldn't my body know just what to do, and it seems like it could be a great, once-in-a-lifetime experience, and it's *my* life, and I want to live it and . . . *and*—"

Celia's eyes are tracking me with the speed a court reporter types with when the key defense witness testifies . . . and . . .

I am living in the land of *and*—the building power of possibility fills me, the flywheel of insight spinning like a washing machine in perfect balance, leaving the mental clothing the cleanest and least wet ever, the dubious task of wringing life out done in an instant of *ands*. I travel to a deep "yes" about my future by allowing pieces of understanding to assemble themselves into a pattern, a weave of reality that is both delicate and strong, a thread that I travel, hand over hand, through uncertain and new territory. I grab this thread, spun from *ands* instead of *buts*, and pull myself along and through.

Celia comments with a humming nod as I speak and catch my breath on the inhales of my *ands*.

"And I am very afraid" falls from my lips, landing loud on the coffee table between us.

"And very excited," she says. "The two emotions feel similar."

"Yes, afraid *and* excited," I say, inspired by the paradox.

"What are you most afraid of?" she asks with the same cool perception as if she just asked where I bought my skirt.

Could she know that I ran down the hall as a girl—as a teen, as an adult maybe, for that is what I am by now—to get a running start, so that I could leap onto my bed to escape the darkness underneath the mattress and the collection of every horror show I should *never, ever* have seen, because I could never *unsee* them? Should I start there or talk about something more relevant . . . a relevant fear? Yet fear has no boundaries and leaks across membranes, bleeding through from one moment to the next, indiscriminate. It is an invisible stalker moving in right next to me on the couch only a millisecond after I declare my spiritual and biological independence from medicalization. I am instantly back in the incubator as a stunned newborn—large and paralyzed.

I share with Celia the story told to me each birthday—of Dory's breech, of the loss of the little girl in between us, and of my mother's emergency C-section when I came into the world.

I trip on my truth. "I am afraid I won't be able to do it. I am afraid that birth and hormones and bone structure are all genetic, and I will have experiences like my mother and almost die." My lower lids fill, and in my mind I run down the hall as fast as I can and take off.

Celia's look and words enter me, mid-jump, rearranging my root ball of reality. "Well, Susanne with an *s,*" she says, the playful specificity of her address adding height to my leap, "the only thing you can inherit from your mother are her fears."

I land in the truth and power of Celia's words, the bed in my mind skidding from the sheer force and momentum of liberty like a surfboard riding a new wave. I breathe in the freedom of this completely brand-new idea. I can be free of the doom of DNA and birth stories. I can release inherited fears. They have no power over me.

. . .

We use legacy to describe a few different concepts in Lightyear. You'll hear the word come up often, so it's important that you deeply understand the concept before we continue.

Think of the dictionary definition of "legacy." First, it can mean a gift or a bequest given to someone. Next, it can be defined as anything handed down from the past. Finally, it can suggest something old or outdated, as in computer hardware that does not work with advanced systems. In Lightyear, legacy means all of these things.

Inherited legacies are the expectations put upon us by our families, our culture, and our world. They are beliefs that limit our behavior. Inherited legacies are ideas such as: Getting married and having children will make you happy, artists will always be poor, or you have to be thin to be successful. Some legacies can be gifts from your parents, some legacies can be obsolete, but all are handed down from the past. Inherited legacies may be true for you and they may not, but it is important to recognize them and make a clear choice about whether or not you want to carry them forward with you. Inherited legacies can center around career, family, gender, socio-economic status, race, or even your health.

Take a moment to think about the legacies you have inherited. What have your parents always wanted for you that you may or may not want to fulfill? What belief has limited you from becoming your true self? These are your inherited legacies and you can choose to release them from your life.

Choice-based legacies are the legacies that you want to bring with you. The core from which you will make decisions in your life. Think of a choice-based legacy as your tagline, something you always come back to. For instance: "I believe that with dedication anything is possible, and I don't need to find my place in the context of a nuclear family in order to feel fulfilled." "I can express my creativity and support myself." "My work is fulfilling and makes me strong, and my body's shape and size has nothing to do with that." These are choice-based legacies that you can choose to carry forward into your life.

Legacy is something that will ripple outward as you interact with the world, whether you're in a conference room or in line at the grocery store. You change others' experiences for better or for worse, and they in turn take that energy and pass it along. Think of legacy not as something you leave behind when you die, but as something you create moment to moment, like footsteps.

Your legacy is never finalized, and every moment is a choice about how you will act and what you will leave behind.

Dr. Jill Bolte Taylor once said, "Please take responsibility for the energy you bring into this space."[1] That responsibility should not be taken lightly.

Here are some examples:

---

1   Jill Bolte Taylor, Ph.D., *My Stroke of Insight* (New York: Penguin Books, May 26, 2009).

INHERITED LEGACIES TO RELEASE

- Artists don't make money.
- Work and life have to be hard.
- To succeed I have to suffer.
- Food will soothe me.
- I can't have/do it all.
- I need to stay quiet to keep the peace.
- I always need more.
- I've got to beat the system.

CHOICE-BASED LEGACIES TO CARRY FORWARD

- I am able to create community through activity.
- I can live a life of service while taking care of myself.
- Fulfillment in all areas of my life is possible.
- I work with intuitive intelligence to get things done.
- I have faith in the current and future generations.
- Work is fun, fulfilling, and abundant.
- I am inquisitive and enjoy looking into the meaning of life.
- Giving without expectation is a way of being.
- Love of people is a renewable resource.

I have found that simply recognizing or *discerning* inherited legacies is the antidote to *judgment*, allowing me to release those legacies that no longer serve me. "Know the truth and the truth will set you free" was the operating adage of Dorothy Wood Espiau and her teachings. I now can sense truth in my body, and so can you if you begin to listen. Each generation has an opportunity and responsibility to honor and care for their lineage by bringing the best forward, forgoing what no longer serves and forgiving any harm that it has done, and integrating what is new.

In most cases, the key to releasing inherited legacies is forgiveness.

Forgiveness does not equal condoning.

Forgiveness is the releasing of carrying the burden, the resentment, the aggravation of not listening or learning earlier. It is a monumental choice of moving forward from a chronic state of unforgiveness, which affords the unforgiver the empty, shabby right to be right about how they or another person are wrong. Unforgiveness is the main character in the drama of duality, and it lives to produce chaos and energy that mimics our positive lifeforce yet has no fulfillment.

As I got older, I released my inherited legacy of fear and all of the associated struggle that reared its head that day. I began to both understand and forgive my mother for her retelling of my traumatic birth. I realize now that she was always attempting to free herself.

Forgiveness is the willingness of the calcified ego to step off the stage of right and wrong, and into a world of unified wholeness. Besides, forgiving *can* be fun. Some days, I wake in a groggy indistinct state of unforgiveness and remind myself, "Oh, right, Suzy . . . remember? You already forgave yourself for that. Stop being a bully to yourself," or "Yeah, girl, remember? You already forgave that business colleague . . . no point wrecking your sweet heart over it. Go to bed, good woman, and rest."

I am pretty sure future generations are thanking me now for tidying up my legacy DNA.

9

Use Your Breath
(But Hold the Garlic)

Del Mar, California
Twenty-Third Street
January 1982

A s life would have it, when I put in my notice with the State of California that I need to leave my post caring for Mrs. Moss because I am having a baby, I believe that is that, and I refer a friend of a friend to take over the role. A few weeks later, I receive a surprise check in the mail for an enormous amount of money—$740! I learn that this is a "disability" payment for being pregnant. The check makes all the difference in the world and will one day become the basis of a Lightyear declaration shared with thousands of young parents: "Babies always bring money."

I use this check plus savings to pay for midwife care with cash, and I sign up for MediCal in case of dire emergency. I develop empathic respect for the social workers that help people get public health services, as it takes me five visits and three months of forms, plus all of my human ability to focus, to qualify, which not even my 4.0 GPA can truly help me with. I comment to my case worker on one visit that I cannot imagine what it would be like to not have a college education and speak English while attempting to do all this paperwork. She lifts her pen from the clipboard and confides that it hurts her to be rendered so ineffective. She'd studied social work to alter the quality of people's lives, but now she moves papers in circles, and has gotten good at telling people to be patient, and has learned how to brace herself for continuing to disappoint the very folk she had imagined serving.

I have never stopped being moved by her, though I do not recall her name. I recall sensing the gap between the picture she had for her life and the one that was actually happening. I sensed her despair and how her heart was on the edge of hardening. I meet people like her every day, at every stage of becoming calcified and altered. I have learned to speak to the living part, to the part that can escape; the part that can resurrect the dream within and regain wholeness. In that moment of her sharing her gap, I was also her, feeling my own disconnect, and powerless to alter her path.

Before I leave Mrs. Moss's, I create an affirmation to help me find a wonderful, affordable home (on the bus line) where I can have a home birth. I use numerology to increase the potency by having all the letters add up to a "6," the number for home, health, and family. I say to myself, hundreds of times per day, "I have a peaceful new place."

These words take me to my newly converted garage home. These words lift me when I am afraid. And yet I do not yet have the courage to say to her, my social worker, there in the dull office filled with forms and lines and signs to nowhere, "Hey, I bet if you hold your picture and create a statement that will support you in times of doubt, you will eventually have a wonderful outcome. That is how I got my home." I do not say those things to her, although I could, and who knows the possible impact.

This capacity to hold a positive picture correlated with words lives as a force to attract a wonderful future into one's life. It is a force as powerful as any I know, helping us hold steady in the face of the-future-that-was-going-to-happen-anyway, otherwise known as our "default" future. Such are the distinctions of Lightyear. Yet there in the social worker's office, I was simply a young experimenter of life and not yet bold enough to share my unschooled discoveries with someone with a master's degree.

My studio apartment comes "furnished" with a dark-brown plaid, overstuffed armchair, a glass-top coffee table, and a Murphy bed that folds into the wall during the daytime. At bedtime, it faces south and out what would have been the garage door and is now an extra-large sliding glass door that spills onto the driveway and Twenty-Third Street. Sleeping in my bed, I can feel where the car might have been.

I revel in my tiny, *private* bathroom with a corner, resin-molded shower, and even though I can barely turn around in the shower or the space at full-term, the solitariness I experience expands the space in my mind.

The shotgun kitchen must be navigated with pre-planning. Opening the fridge, or a cupboard, or a drawer means skooching way back, or turning sideways and reaching for the desired thing with one arm and a semi-squat. A line dance of purpose and agility is part of everyday cooking. A pot of vegetarian chili is ever ready on the top shelf as whole protein and as something readily available after coming home from school. Stir-fry ingredients, cheese, apples, carrot juice, a German brand of liquid iron, and a host of nut butters, including tahini, create, over time, a baby. I marvel at how I never needed to know how to differentiate a liver cell from a heart cell, and "make" things happen. Never did I need to say to my body, "Okay, here is the template for the next step. Your deadline is . . ." Quite the contrary. A deep, silent genius is at work.

On the kitchen counter, an open case of Heinekens with two bottles missing rests, awaiting her next takers. My father visited a few days ago and bought them for me. "Beer is a food group for Germans, and it will help your milk come in." All of it is curious and true, intimate and telling. The last thing I actually need is a case of Heinekens, yet their presence, a marker of my father's visit, is a comfort. The dozen red roses he gave me three days ago for Valentine's Day are in full expression on the table beside the chair.

I sit in the deep lap of my plaid armchair, taking in the long, slow breath of a full-term woman. I have completed a photography project, and have it spread out on the floor at my feet. I pull myself forward to look beyond my belly and see the set of images I have shot of my shoes (a pair of men's Topsiders), along with the sheep-fur baby moccasins Mom gave me for the baby to come, balancing on a 2 x 4 floating in the runoff near the nearby tracks. I am shooting closer to home these days, literally and figuratively. I am looking for ways to leverage my assignments with something I want for my own life. These are not my best images—the negatives overexposed, the prints grainy. Yet I love them. There is something about the shoes, representing both of us, and there we are balancing on a piece of wood in a mirrored reflection.

The phone is beside the plaid chair, which is my new command center. In an earlier phone call with my mom, when I first moved into the garage house, I let her know about my decision to work with the San Diego Midwives. I said, "Hey, Mom, I wanted you to know I studied all the options, and I've decided to hire a team of midwives, Celia and Ally, to assist with the birth. You would like them. They are very kind and knowledgeable."

"What does that mean? They come to the hospital with you?"

"No, it means they come to my house, and I have the baby here. It means I have a home birth."

Silence and then a breath.

"Jesus Christ!" Mom utters, with extended emphasis on the Jesus part.

"Exactly, He was born in a stable!"

"Jesus Christ!" she retorts to my sassy comeback. "Jesus Christ." I feel my mother both resist my decision and accept it as mine. Like we were crossing some body of water, with the shoes representing each of us, and now, instead of only mother and daughter, a new geometry has emerged of two adults inside of the original pattern, yet altogether different and changed.

"Jesus Christ, Suzy . . . okay. I love you. I'm sending your dad to visit."

"I love you too, Mom. Everything will be fine."

And so, out of that conversation, I got a reconnaissance visit from my dad to check on the safety and overall well-being of my new home, a case of beer, and a bouquet of roses. Dad reports after his visit that I am indeed fine.

· · ·

Waist deep in the ocean, the wave is sucking me back from the shore ahead of me and into its enormous face, high and loud. Its crest covers me completely in dark gray bubbles, the sound muffled, and I lose all footing. I am pushed to the other side by a blow to the head and held under. I tumble, my arms and legs whipped by the power of the water, my movements mute and fruitless as I fail to reach the surface.

With no breath left, I am in full survival mode, punctuated by a fleeting moment of wonder as time stops.

"Is this how I die?" Time restarts. My face comes to the surface, but not through my own efforts, and the wave rescinds and releases me for a moment. I take in the air, yet as much saltwater enters me as breath. My eyes sting and bulge, my lungs burning as I choke, only to have more air and water meet the back of my throat.

"Yes, this is how, this is where, this is now." I slip out above myself, like stepping out of a silk nightgown, and I slide from one place to another without struggle. Lifting a few feet, I see above the waves my body tumbling on the surface, then held under again. On the shore, a brown, strong young man, yet older than me, perhaps in his thirties, muscular and tattooed with a full beard and mustache, impeccably trimmed, walks calmly to the edge of the sea. The foam of the white wash moves around his feet. He continues walking, not swimming, into the surf, paced and secure, with each step delivering him closer, as if he were on land instead of heading directly into perilous surf.

He extends one leveraged arm into the wave currently tossing my body, takes hold of me, and, as if with pure intention and not brawn, lifts me out of the water and onto the shore. My awareness above the water reintegrates with my mostly drowned self and I recognize I am in a dream yet still sleeping. Lying on the sand, he kneels beside me, looking at me with brown eyes as calm as his feet a moment earlier when he approached the waves and my near death. There are no words. Only a look. A seeing. Pure love. A transcendent knowing and assurance. I see now that he is older than me. Stronger, wiser, protective.

The shock of living wakes me from the dream. I am back on the Murphy bed.

The scene plays in the theater of my mind on repeat, and always to rest again on the ending note of wordless greater love. The wisdom within tells me I have met my son.

I rise with my stomach growling to pee, drink water, and then tuck myself back into bed, knowing the photography project is due tomorrow. Sleep comes.

I awake with a sharp pain, followed by a dull one. It is still dark. I fumble to find my watch. It is one of the Casios Suranjith bought at Costco that first summer in 1980 to trade for hash with monks on the Pakistani border. The watch is fully modern, electronic, glow-in-the-dark, and *plastic*—not a heavy, weighted gold-and-silver-colored metal watch. The monks would heft the watch in one hand, measuring both its weight and value in a method similar to the one they applied to measure the worth of the hash: like for like. The ultra-light Casios had no value in the high Himalayas, and so this one made it back to the States to become my watch.

Suranjith has been gone four months, since October 7. I receive occasional, translucent letters written in Suranjith's tiny script in pen on specially created USPS one-page, tri-folding, self-adhesive, preprinted postage airmail letter format. These I cherish and reread often, as if in the rereading of these letters, there will be a new message, something like "Suzy, I love you. I am returning to the U.S. and plan to go to school and become someone who can support a family. I miss you and see how fun and intelligent you are. It must be intense and challenging to be going through what you are going through." Yet that is not what the letters say, ever.

They are written in phases—I can tell by the different pens used or the texture of what he had been writing on: a smooth desk, a wooden grain table, or nubby concrete. Changes in his mood and intention are evident. I can and do see all of this, and in seeing what I see, I quickly hide the seeing from myself. Much of the letters are about "Why are you not sending me money?" *Isn't it obvious?* I think, but clearly it is not obvious to him. Obvious is not always obvious.

So my Casio glows in the dark with the touch of a side button. 3:44 a.m.

I gather my mind and sensations. On my last visit to see Celia, I was already fully effaced, and one centimeter dilated, and that was a few days ago. I could be beginning labor, yet it is too early to call Veronica, so I wait. Ally has told us over and over again, "Get as much rest as you can. You do not know how long your labor will go. Birth is about stamina, and stamina comes from rest."

I lie back down on my Murphy bed, yet my nervous system is christened with a mindful high alert of adrenaline, and I hold my watch in my hand like a small, comforting stuffed animal, my thumb over its face.

4:06 a.m.

Dear God. A pattern.

Here we go.

Dull droning and tightening grow in intensity and fall off slowly, and I know these are not Braxton-Hicks contractions. Hungry, yet not hungry, I am almost nauseated yet not as I experience these sensations like nothing I know, yet I know them now. I am educated instantly, receiving a transmission from the entire millennium of human existence directly to me without study or practice.

Eat. Eat now. Eat now before you can't. Eat. Eat now. Girl, get yourself up and eat!

The voices of my ancestors chant and I must concede.

I rise in the darkness, slip on my wooden clogs, and find my way to my hall-of-a-kitchen. I flip on the bright florescent lights without dimmers, scattering the beach roaches I have learned to incorporate into gracious Del Mar beach living. I pull Ezekiel bread, eggs, raw cream-on-the-top milk, and butter from the fridge, doing my squat twist maneuver. Then I reach to the cupboard for honey, cinnamon, and tahini. Yes, this is what I make for my Last Breakfast. French toast with honey tahini and bananas. The honey and tahini combination might as well be halvah, the Middle Eastern dessert, which I have discovered at Windmill Farms. Yet, because I create it, my meal falls into the breakfast, not dessert category. Besides, I have just survived near drowning.

The egg-and-cinnamon-drenched bread hits the sizzling butter as droplets skittle on the pan, sending a puff of heaven into the air. I reach for the spatula and lose my centeredness to a pinching within that radiates quickly into the third proper set of contractions. Determined to complete my task, I steady myself on the handle of the range and breathe as the heat does its work on the bread. Sliding the spatula underneath the bread, I see the edge, browned and splotched just right, and flip it with ease. Side two of the French toast belly-flops on the skillet squarely. The sound wet bread makes early in the morning when all edges hit the pan at once is like cupped palms coming together, hollow yet certain.

I am aware of how aware I am becoming. Like the knobs on the gas stove, the dials of my sensation are set on high. The once-delightful smells are overbearing, and I open the back door to stand in the cool of the dark winter morning. The marine condensate forms droplets that descend from the roof, a few landing on the top of my head. They surprise me.

Turning back into the hall kitchen, butter smoke has gathered above the skillet, and despite the smell, my inner safety officer self deftly recovers my Last Breakfast from near incineration. Dark brown. It is the kind of dark brown that is healthy—an eating-activated-charcoal kind of healthy—like the kind you put in a fish aquarium filter and wonder how it all works kind of healthy. And so it is that my Last Breakfast fully represents all things: the golden side of the Larsons, the dark brown of the Gablins, the homemade halvah (because it tastes so good), and the cinnamon and bananas of Sri Lanka.

I do not eat it, though.

At least not for another twenty minutes.

Instead, I go back to the command center chair and consider sitting and find that walking through the contractions works better.

Veronica is the One Voice. The person who has stepped up and stepped in with love and without agenda to help me with this baby. I do not question this. It makes sense to me. Like a group of kids saying, "Hey, I've got a guitar and you've got a keyboard. Wanna start a band?" Spontaneous, creative, unfolding, yet perhaps predestined? "Hey, I've got a baby in me and you've got the ability and love. Wanna come over for my home birth?"

Veronica lives with her mother, and an early phone call will wake up everyone.

I call.

I wake them up.

Veronica arrives in her mother's car. She brings extra pillows because her mother said, "You never know how many pillows you will need."

The sun is coming up now, and so is the next wave of contractions.

. . .

It's now sometime later, who knows how much later—my rational mind is not in charge—and all I know is that every time the contractions come, they come longer, harder, and closer together. This is exactly what all the books say, yet the observation of it and the being-in-it-of-it are two very different things. I am not able to stabilize my mind and say, "Hello, Susanne, your labor is progressing exactly as planned and you are on the correct trajectory." No. None of these thoughts are here.

I am on the Murphy bed, on my side, breathing as if my life depends on it. My life does depend on it, this I know intellectually, yet breathing is now saving my life. It is my life. I took my running start to leap over the demons under the bed, only to land *in* the bed, swirling in fear in a swamp of dark, sticky energy, its tentacles on my throat, slipping inside me, and talking to me from within: "You are dying."

Liz, the assistant midwife, arrives. Veronica has been in communication with Celia, but because first babies often take a while—often upwards of eighteen hours—Liz is on the first wave of support. She is buoyant, eager, and has a head of dark, curly hair. Unfortunately, she has made an incredibly poor choice somewhere in the last twenty-four hours. To all aspiring doulas, midwifes, and well-wishers of women in labor: learn from Liz. Learn now, and it could be the whole reason you read this book; you must say to your children and their children's children, and pass down this wisdom of the ages, this torch of truth to guide the well-being of the birth process. You must say with heart and emphasis: "Dear Ones, listen. *Never* eat garlic before you attend to a laboring woman." People will listen to you, and you will save millions from the fear of this:

I am now on my other side, propped by the multitude of pillows from Veronica's mom's house, my eyes closed to focus on my breathing, the lifeline fragile between this world and the next, while Liz sits beside me so close her weight shifts my position, bringing her face within inches of mine. Before she even speaks, she radiates a pore-drenched assault of garlic, and my focus stutters. I lose the tiny handhold I possess on the cliff and tumble in an irreversible free fall of enormous physical pain and even greater soul pain. "I am dying. I can't do this." The words tumble within me and become more and more true as I collect evidence during my devastating descent that these must be the fear-filled sensations of imminent death.

"How are you doing?" Liz asks this with the heart of innocence and the breath of Agent Orange or Napalm or any other chemical weapon of mass destruction.

Now, completely overcome, I cannot speak, or breathe, or live. That's it.

She speaks again. "Let's check your vitals."

"No, dear God, please make her stop speaking," I plead within.

Liz sits up to get her bag of instruments and I am flooded with the instant relief of a prayer answered. "If I can just keep her away from my face," I strategize, as if my life depends upon it.

She places the Doppler on my rock-hard belly and gets the baby's heartbeat. *All good.* Next, a vaginal exam to see how far dilated I am. Thank God, she is away from my face.

"Whoa!" Liz says, then catches herself. Veronica and Liz whisper and confer.

I close my eyes and continue breathing. I am teaching myself how to keep the rest of my body relaxed when my uterus contracts. I start with relaxing my jaw, and as long as I don't smell garlic, I can do it.

I hear Liz on the phone with Celia. "Yes, you better get here right now. She's fully dilated. Yes . . . No . . . Yes . . . I don't know. The other thing is, her water has not broken, and the amniotic sac is sticking out . . . Really? Okay . . . I've never done that before . . . When will you get here? Okay . . . God." Liz returns from the command center plaid chair to stand by the bed. I sense she is more afraid than I am. Veronica, although fully untrained, has a natural way of being with whatever is happening. She moves through life without judgment or attachment, creating a space of warmth and safety by sheer instinct.

"Suzy, she's going to need to break your waters," Veronica says. "It would be nice if we could leave the sac be and let Celia get here, yet that's not the way it's going down. When they break, things will get more intense. You're doing great." Veronica shares all of it. Truth, surrender, validation. She holds my hand. She has not eaten any garlic.

I never got to eat my burnt French toast.

A gush of warmth and wetness overtakes me, and there is a shift in pressure, a new grittiness and tightness. With no ledge left to balance on, no pretense of control on any level or any dimension, I begin to push.

Liz says, "You can push now!" asserting her unsynchronized authority.

"Duh," I say playfully to myself, having just enough energy to remain internally snarky.

My jaw clenches, my molars taut against each other, and my lungs hold tight to their air, burning everywhere, within and without. To limit the sensory input, my eyes close, and I again see myself lifting out, just as I had in my dream. This time it is different. I see myself here on the Murphy bed, safe on a raft, knowing that I am both the dream and the dreamer, united and differentiated all at once. A flash of rest fleets through me, instantaneously eternal, and I cry out, my mouth open with moaning—a sound long and low.

"Aweooooooooppppppennnn." *Open.* I inhale deeply and richly to the bottom like a bellows preparing for the forge. Again, I cry out. Until now I have been a silent laborer, internal and focused, but here I am, gutturally singing. I am guided from within and aligning language with action. *Open. Open, Open.* Like a rower getting in sync with the current, my resistance drops to zero and the speed compounds. I feel the full rushing of air expressing and resonating in my throat, and the note saves my life. *Open.*

"Whoa!" Liz says in her best Southern Californian on the inhale. "This baby's here!"

I am facing the side door and in rushes Celia just as the baby crowns, and she deftly joins Liz as a million things go right.

· · ·

Breath is as underrated as forgiveness. Often, we only care about it when our heads are underwater. As the current-day, inspirational hip-hop preacher Eric Thomas said: "When you want to succeed as bad as you want to breathe, then you'll be successful."[2]

> *Breath is the great communicator*
> *between body and spirit.*

It is our personal conversation with the immediate and the eternal. It is prana, life force. Learning to become aware of, work with, and control our breath is the deepest and simplest form of self-leadership. The wisest one-word sentence? "Breathe."

As I've jokingly said, it is better to have bad breath than no breath.

---

2   Eric Thomas, *Secret to Success* (Snellville, GA: Spirit Reign Publishing, 2011).

Always remember, as long as we are still breathing, it is never too late to have a new beginning.

There are many sound resources—both modern and ancient—for breath training and exercises, which the ardent among you will readily find. In earnest, I must share that in this realm I am self-taught, a disciple of my own experiences, and not trained by Hindu or Tibetan masters. Here are a few things I offer:

For all birthing mothers, in addition to the garlic ban for any attendant, I include the little known "exhale pushing" breathing method. The tendency to hold the breath instead of *using* the breath to move deep sensation, whether physical, emotional, or other, is where most people get stuck. There are many birthing scenes in films that depict the woman holding her breath, lying on her back, and bearing down. These three things together make giving birth harder than if gravity and breath could be integrated. Exhale on the push and vocalize in some way. If possible, say "open." If possible, move, sit up, or squat.

For people who are birthing other things— new ideas, important conversations, growing companies, new ways of living—the tendency can also be to hold the breath unconsciously, to perhaps not use posture that can help, and stop saying what we need, as we need it. We can, like the birthing mother, interpret the intense body sensations as pain—that "something is wrong"—instead of using our breath to move positive energy into the natural discomfort of growth and change. Breath, posture, movement and singing, or speaking our most essential theme allow a million things to go right.

Breath is here to help us birth ourselves anew with each cycle.

10

Watch for Melbas

Del Mar, California
Fall 1981

Every other week since Suranjith left for Sri Lanka in October, a woman named Melba has come either on her own or with one of her friends, picked me up in her car, and taken me to lunch at the vegetarian place near Swami Beach and the Self-Realization Fellowship Center in Encinitas. For this, I am very grateful, as I do not have the funds to go out to eat, and having Melba around has been like a visit with my own grandmother. She asks me how I am feeling, and how my classes are going, and if I like toasted garbanzo beans. She makes my life feel stable and simple—the stuff of ladies who lunch while enjoying each other's company.

This kind of freedom, which existed between my mom and me in high school, is now gone, and our conversations, when they happen, are tactical or filled with her heavy, unresolved worry and statements of concern. It is not that I misunderstand her, I just need a conversational lunch every now and then. Melba provided rhythm to the weeks of my pregnancy in the way that I provided rhythm to Mrs. Moss's days with her Pepperidge Farm jelly and cream cheese sandwiches.

Suranjith met Melba many months ago in line at the Vista DMV of all places. As the story goes, they got to talking and had similar interests. Melba and her friends were Rosicrucians. I had never heard of Rosicrucians before, yet I can tell you that the ones I've met are very nice people. What I've sorted out, and this is by no means the total depth and reality of their practice, is that Rosicrucians are Christians that believe in reincarnation and astrology. That was enough to pique a conversation worthy of follow-up for a man like Suranjith, raised in a deeply Catholic family by his Hindu aunt.

And so the DMV line up brought Melba into my life, even though Suranjith was out of it. Mostly.

. . .

A few months before I give birth, I am in the passenger seat of Melba's car, watching as her hands grip the wheel at ten and two o'clock. She drives sensibly on the thoroughfares from Del Mar to Vista instead of the freeway, her large, plastic-framed glasses sliding down her nose with an occasional adjustment from her left middle finger. Her fine hair of many colors of gray, long enough to cover her ears and not her neck, blows softly with the A/C. She is slender and wears simple slacks that are too big. Why women over sixty do this, I do not know. Her tunic comes below where it wants to. Melba is on the short side, so her tunic has more of a skirt feeling. Her eyes are chipper and alert, her voice high and a bit crackled, her energy vital, and her mood bright. We are driving to her home for the first time and she is making me lunch. She asked permission to read my chart during our last visit. I agreed and she has prepared it.

Pulling into her driveway, I see an American flag flying from a brass pole near the front door. The nondescript houses are attached and finished with the beige stucco the homeowners association covenants require. Like seeing the outside of an abalone shell, dull and protective, we then enter through the threshold of the door opening to the world of Melba—iridescent and pearly. Books, chimes, china, small photographs, and miniature oil paintings adorn her home with the sense of individual history and love.

Our conversations have never been deep, and she tends to turn the direction back to me, but I have learned that once she was married and her husband has passed. She also has a son named Jamie that she adopted or fostered, and it is clear Jamie struggles in life. From what little Melba has said about Jamie, her love is clear and her impact variable.

"Oh, he's bouncing around a bit right now, you know?" she tells me.

What she's shared of Jamie's life is not new to me. I have my university life surrounded by people with futures, affluence, direction, support, and second chances. Then there are the people I have met through Veronica and her friends and family. I see directly their struggle to make enough money to pay rent, the staccato efforts to go to community college at night, or in the day if they clean office on the graveyard. People at counters in 7-Elevens, service stations, the taco stands. Then there are the people that buy hash from Suranjith—good people, good addicts, good customers. It would be cultural misappropriation to call Suranjith a dealer. He sells hash to cover costs and to cover dreams such as flying home to Sri Lanka for "business trips." By now, in Southern California at least, this lifestyle of living marginally, pain buffeted by pot, and living check to check is so normalized that films are being made about it.

A light moves across Melba's face, as if it's always been there and the shadow covering it is lifting. I come to understand this is the face of worry. I see it on the faces of many people. It is the gateway face to resignation. I have not seen this face on Melba before. She hands me a small framed photo of a young man with dark hair and a mustache, possibly Hispanic or Italian or Middle Eastern. He is handsome, yet stern-looking for a young person.

"That's him." She inhales slowly. I see for the first time a sunkenness in her cheeks and darkness under her eyes. "This is from a few years ago."

Without knowing the whole story, or even needing to know the whole story, I say, "He looks to be a good person and one who will find his way, even if it takes time, and it's not a straight line."

We both giggle. If Melba did have a message she wanted to impart during our veggie luncheons, it was that nothing happens in a straight line and that the spiral is our friend.

We talk about this and that, the color of roses, how wide the streets are, whether Nancy and Ronald Reagan miss California weather, the sound of aircraft overhead, the price of fruit in the winter, which house plants love the sun, which ones need the shade, and we attempt to answer more pressing questions, such as: Just how much fur does a cat shed in a year?

Later, with the food eaten, table cleared, and water glasses set, Melba retrieves a pile of books and papers from another room and sets them down with the focus of a suburban alchemist, navigating centuries of wisdom and decades of place mats. Her gray-blue eyes meet mine, and for a moment, she touches me with these words. "This is why I asked you here. I have read your chart and I thought you ought to know. You will work with radioactivity." This surprises me, as I have not shared with Melba anything about my father's work. "And when it is needed most," she tells me, "you will help bring millions out of fear." I sit quietly and process how absurd yet real her words feel.

. . .

Del Mar, California
Twenty-Third Street
February 1982

Melba comes to visit three days after Surya is born. Now that the birth and its uncertainties are over, Mom has flown out from D.C. to help me. Melba's friend Vera must have driven her this time, as I do not recognize the car in the driveway facing into our living room. Mom and I situate Melba in the plaid chair and swaddle Surya up for her to hold him.

Newborn babies are mystical. Surya is round, brown, alert, and perfect in every way. Tiny "skid marks" on the sides of his forehead from the "precipitous" (let's just call it "speedy") birth are the only marks of his journey. His head has soft brown hair so snuggle-worthy. Melba is proud, delighted, and beams even with her eyes closed as she brings him to her shoulder, rocking slowly from side to side.

"He's beautiful, isn't he, Trula?" Melba turns to Mom, sharing this as a truth more than a question.

"Yes, he is," Mom says. Mom is excellent help these first days, and she has put the hustle on to get the place picked up and ready for guests, in addition to going to the coin laundry with all the baby and adult clothes that get covered with poo, pee, spit-up, blood, leaking milk, and whatnot.

After seven minutes of "Look at his hands" and "How was your flight out?" and "Has your milk come in?" and "Are you getting some sleep?" Melba announces, "Well, I'd better let you rest." She hands Surya to Mom and, rising to hug me goodbye, brings my head to hers with her hand, much like she did with the baby, and whispers to me, "Remember what I told you, Susanne." Vera takes Melba by the elbow and they step through the sliding glass door and out to their car.

Two days later, Vera calls to let me know that Melba died the day after their visit.

I am not sad or overly sentimental about Melba's death and, in retrospect, I could have seen that she had some type of heart disease from the blueness of her fingernails. I did not know Melba deeply, and she was only in my life for a very brief time, and I did not know her motives. Yet what I've experienced is her consistent and specific concern for me as expressed through lunches, visits, and a Rosicrucian, astrological, over-tomato-and-cheese-sandwiches reading.

It is not until I have my first job at the Department of Energy in five years that I will even remember what she told me that afternoon in her home. I feel the tangible effect of being watched over, of being delivered, of being held. I knew Melba for about the same amount of time as I did Celia and her team of midwives, who also supported me with consistent observation and nurtured me without judgment.

I have come to learn that people can enter our lives with very specific purposes, missions, and gifts that support our journey to becoming our own hero in life.

Can I say with proof that Melba extended her life to see Surya come into the world? No. Yet you may have discerned by now that "proof" is of malleable value. Melba taught me to watch for Melbas. To watch for miracles, angels, messages, sandwiches, and provisions of all dimensions. She taught me the immediacy of love.

So I am not sad or sentimental for this reason: She is still with me, handing me vegetarian sandwiches and whispering encouragement to get the job done.

. . .

I enrolled in the winter quarter knowing full well I would have a baby in the middle. Who does that? Well, I did. I stacked my classes on Tuesdays and Thursdays to give myself time to do odd jobs and prepare the studio for a baby. Surya is born on a Wednesday, I skip class on Thursday (imagine that) and Mom flies in, Melba visits on Saturday, my milk comes in, Mom buys a rocker from the unfinished furniture store on Monday, and I get the call from Vera learning that Melba has passed while sitting in the new rocking chair.

"You need to get back to class, Suzy," Mom says on Tuesday, as if she is living my life and knows best. Yet that is the most-often-used color within the mom-speak spectrum—ask any child.

"Oh, I can miss a week, Mom. I'm already ahead on my work and—"

"You need to go," she says without further consideration. Granted, she is likely as sleep-deprived as I am, with both of us sleeping on the Murphy bed taking turns with Surya in the rocker.

I do not need to be a psychic to read that there is only one way this is going. Although not expressed as actual words, I can feel her worry that I will become a college dropout, scavenge for subservient secretarial jobs, and basically run amok.

Tuesday is here and my destiny is written on my mother's brow. She is determined I will not miss "Women Studies: A Film Retrospective," one of the communications electives I've chosen in hopes that it would be easy enough to accomplish with a baby and buffer the direct hits that would come my way from Organic Chemistry and other pre-med requirements. I've shifted from Communications and Visual Arts into Public Health and pre-Med courses, with the backup idea of becoming a physician as a single mother. The pregnancy thrust many survival-based plans my way, including and not limited to: entering medical school. I know I have the grades and I figure I can make enough money once I graduate. In a moment of sanity during the next school year, the wonderful mentor Dr. Barbara guides me into preventative Public Health policy, saying to me in words that shape my life, "Susanne, with communication skills like yours, help people *before* they get sick and need a doctor."

We pile into Mom's rental for Surya's second car ride. The first one was to the University Hospital to test for PKU, a debilitating condition that if caught early is fully correctable. This was a test that the midwives recommended we do, especially as the incidence rate is higher in "Islanders," and we figured that, since Sri Lanka is an island, why risk it?

That trip felt like Homer's *Odyssey*, both Homer's experience and the reader's. I was unable to estimate the culture shock of leaving a small, loving space like the converted garage studio for a public institution. All three of us returned exhausted from the pressures of the external world—things like navigating, parking, waiting rooms in the public health system, explaining why Surya was not born in a hospital to the nurse who had strong opinions to share without edit, and talking to the guy my age who had both his legs in full-length casts because he was sleeping on Mission Beach and got run over by a truck. He wore rolled-up Hawaiian-print surf shorts and a loose Hang Ten t-shirt, and hadn't shaved for days. His brown whiskers turned red in the light when the direct winter morning sun came through the office. He was polite and funny to all three of us and the whole brief encounter forevermore gave new meaning to the saying "I feel like I've been hit by a truck."

This second trip would be longer.

(It's early 1982 and infant car seats will not become mandatory until 1985. I only know this now because I've looked it up on the internet. What I know at the time is that because I don't have a car, I don't need to think about it, yet with Mom and me and Surya in the rental car, new geometries are required.)

We provision our car with a beer cooler with a bottle of breast milk and a Fresca, baby blankets, pillows, cloth diapers, pre-moistened wash cloths in plastic bags, an extra set of clothes, and a tiny, stuffed toy camel for good company. I swaddle Surya up and hold him in my arms in the passenger's seat and we head out of Twenty-Third Street and into the world.

My mother's driving skills have only sharpened with a few years of experience in our nation's capital. Once—Dad told me this, not Mom—she became frustrated by the traffic on the Memorial Bridge, backed her car onto the shoulder, and took herself off in reverse gear for hundreds of yards like in a James Bond film. Undoubtedly, that kind of maneuver is illegal yet effective, and Dad was proud of his wife and said things like "Your mother could duel with a Puerto Rican cab driver."

And so it is that Surya and I bond our fate in the front seat with a woman who duels with Puerto Rican cab drivers.

We turn left onto the Pacific Coast Highway heading south, first along the beautiful log-strewn beach and then upwards to the Torrey Pines Cliffs where the view of the Pacific Ocean is a magical blend of gray to blue to a thin line of reflective white, then the sky above it mirrors back the blue and then gray.

My belly is still that of a pregnant woman. People tell you these things yet no one, including me, listens. Why would we? In birth class they tell you all the stuff that will happen before, during, and after, yet the gap between conceptual knowledge and actually knowing is as vast as my view of the Pacific.

My belly is distended and my flat, Norwegian alpine long-distance skier breasts are now the double-D thieves of good posture, curving my shoulders in and over. They tingle with a life of their own, communicating through unseen means, through chemical messages, scents of need directed seemingly by the baby, directly bypassing my college-trained mind. My uterus, on the other hand, contracts so severely when the baby nurses that my stomach turns with the memory of birth. Again, without a vote or even a proxy from my mental mind.

School. School. School.

Right-handed, one-sided desks attached to fiberglass-molded chairs that I barely could fit in towards the end await me in every classroom. They are rigid, loud, and unforgiving. We pass the Scripps Clinic, white and iconic and somewhat smart-assed. I feel spaced out and insufficient in my black Indian print skirt and ruffled blouse with easy nursing access. Could this be the sensation cattle have when they follow the inevitable path to the slaughterhouse? Researchers wonder why they do not retaliate, while others postulate that the cows are too dumb and don't know. Others offer that they are so smart, and because they know, they submit as if they are sedated earlier than needed.

I felt this way when I wanted to get away from Suranjith, and here it is again. A plodding, purposeless destiny, a muffling of sensation. A false surrender. This is not about my mother and her conviction about me finding a way to finish college. This is about . . . what is this about? My mental thread falters and I find myself in a fog. Do I nap right here in the car? Do I hope it passes? Is it hormonal? Am I losing too much blood? Should I tell Mom? Is this normal?

I would learn many, many years later what this sensation is fore-telling. It is the sensation of assimilation.

Assimilation is the loss of individuality.

Many people teach, "We are all One." "Well, one what?" I ask. One glob of mass-conscious beliefs marching without question to create the same pains and problems of the generation before? A numbing, gentle clubbing of the unique aspects of growth, tamping them back into the soil?

We are set on the Earth to be the only being we can be, 100 per-cent ourselves, distinct in our contributions, gifts, and purposes.

Our car turns sharply right at the green light, likely faster than the speed limit, and I snap into sudden awareness that I am on a one-way highway—Mom is careening to campus and there is no turning back. It is school or nothing. Nothing about my situation fits what the uni-versity offers. I am now an outlier in a formula to educate that has no space in the margins to doodle with newborns.

We park in the vastness of the Muir College lots. Ignition off. The sun approaches the horizon. Wintery light diffusing through the dusty windshield, Mom puts her right hand on my left knee, throttling it and declaring, "Give me the baby and go." We are early. People with relatives from Wisconsin are always early. I don't want to leave the car, no less Surya. This is our first time separated by a dis-tance greater than the hypotenuse of my apartment.

Walking up the first flight of stairs alone, my maxi-*maxi* birth-blood pad that feels like a giant diaper moves from side to side as I trudge along, feeling a great gush of warmth move into it, and aston-ishingly, through it. Trip one to the bathroom. "Good thing you were early," I hear my mom say in my head. "Good thing you were pre-pared," I hear again.

The classroom fills up with over fifty students—girls in hoodies, some with long sweater cardigans, rows dotted with the few boys that circle the early eighties Women's Studies curriculum circuit. I wonder what the Men's Studies curriculum looks like. Florescent lights bring out the green and red in all our faces and provide an unflattering equality. The sun makes her way down past the ocean.

I don't feel well.

Yet a sound within me—like the song a mother whale sings to locate her baby, a vibrational cellular pull—calls to me, soothing the ragged discord of unbelonging I feel in the classroom. This pull allows me to become larger somehow, large as the ocean itself, inclusive of her continents. The voice of the professor fades, the light becomes diffused, milk engorging my breasts, letting down and saturating my bra and shirt, blood filling the second pad.

I see Melba's thin, blue smile reminding me, "When it is needed most, you will help bring millions out of fear." Perhaps the millions are my own cells? I chuckle—kind, internal, alive, and deeply in love with the power of perspective.

Be early. Be prepared. Watch for Melbas.

· · ·

Along our lifespan there are Melbas—people who see us, believe in us, and give us signposts at particular junctures or inflection points. I did not give much thought to Melba's prophecy that I would work with radioactivity or help bring millions out of fear. I dismissed it as unmerited maternal affection until I found myself, five years later, in the former Atomic Energy Commission building. Even though my mind was muddied with personal failure, student debt, betrayal, and plenty of fear, I recalled our special lunch, her emphatic dramatic proclamation, her melting into baby Surya, and her early death.

Can you magnify the voices of the Melbas? The people who see you in the big picture, living and giving on a larger level? Can you let *that* information in and allow your *purpose* to be mentored while dismissing the voices of fear, doubt, and worry? Take your skills and do more. Think bigger. Help in a grander way in your community.

This is our task. This is the ambitious ask.

11

Invite Wisdom to Pull Up a Chair

Germantown, Maryland

Spring 1987

I park my 1977 Volvo with its balding tires and inoperative radio, and march towards the front door of the building in my sensible pumps, L'eggs pantyhose, and shoulder pads in my neutral navy skirt suit. My thick, Norwegian blonde hair—about five pounds of it—is pulled back in a braid, leaving it a lethal registered weapon in seven states if I swing my head fast to one side.

Freshly plucked from my West Coast failed life, I ready myself to enter the former Atomic Energy Commission offices, now the Department of Energy offices. The building was constructed during the 1950s, twenty-three miles from what was then known as "Ground Zero"—the District of Columbia. The distance from the nation's capital took into account that the largest conceivable weapon at the time was twenty megatons (the bomb dropped on Hiroshima was less than one megaton). The building was specially designed with the idea that people would be safe here in Germantown if D.C. is ever under direct nuclear attack. *Comforting.*

Shoulder pads and pantyhose will not be enough to protect me from what is to come.

I walk into the screening area for my first meeting with my new client—the Defense Waste Management Department of the Department of Energy (DOE). You see, the whole world is pivoting into a new reality. The DOE had been sued for not complying with federal environmental laws that govern hazardous wastes such as benzene or volatile organic compounds. A new world of transparency and openness awaits, or at least that is the stated goal.

I am pivoting into a new reality as well. No more walks on the sandy beaches of North San Diego County with my little family, which now includes two small boys. I've failed to find a way to support them, and my husband Sunji has not been here to help or provide; he has indeed been a vast economic, emotional, and spiritual liability. Yet here I am on the perimeter of my future, entering the threshold of a place designed by the minds of the likes of Dr. Strangelove and maybe worse.

Wearing a plastic badge and lanyard about my neck, I am checked and cross-checked by an armed guard, his eyes already glazed by the routine of his task at only 7:45 in the morning. I realize he is likely on the last fifteen minutes of his night shift.

My body tightens in my heart and through my stomach—mind jumpy. With my shift about to begin, I cross-examine myself. *How did I get here? Who are these people? Where do I belong in any of this?*

The guard startles me with "Miss?"

I reach in the pocket of my blazer, retrieving the folded sheet of paper confirming the time and location of my appointment, and show it to him.

"Follow the arrows to the elevator and take it down to the basement."

I nod with wide eyes, wondering if he can see that I am a West Coast person trapped in an East Coast outfit.

"Follow the numbers to the office," he guides me. "There are a lot of turns. That's how they built this place."

I gather my shiny, deep-plum leather briefcase and walk down the hall. The paint on the walls is thick and the same color yellow they talk about in college psychology texts describing the studies done in the 1950s on subjects in mental asylums. Apparently, pale yellow calms the criminally insane. I wonder if the experiments were done here.

The offices in the basement are, by definition, windowless. The halls echo and bounce the sounds of roller carts carrying files, elevators descending and ascending, the omnipresent buzz of fluorescent ceiling lights, and the voices of men. As I pass by offices, I see a flashing door frame of visual detail: black-and-white framed, yet indistinct, 8 x 10 photos covering the walls inside each office in what appear to be a timed sequence, like how a mother would frame school photos year by year and hang them in a tidy, progressive line.

I enter the office at the end of the hall on the left and meet Fred, my new client, the man in charge, or *maybe* in charge, of the contract that Braddock, Dunn & McDonald (BDM) has with the Department of Energy. I am an entry-level "associate" at BDM earning $23,000 annually, working for what the industry calls "Beltway Bandits," the stream of souls that do the work for the government on contract without being actual government employees. This is one of the outcomes of Reaganomics, a tactic to reduce "big government" and then put the rough stuff out to bid. We are still eighteen months away from the November 1988 presidential elections and riding the wave of outsourced everything. I am part of a team of people hired to make recommendations to amend Department of Energy regulations regarding their internal handling of hazardous and radioactive waste. The DOE are responding to a whole host of lawsuits, and they need manpower to show that they are changing their ways. They have to show progress or risk having their operations shut down.

I've come to work for BDM as a soon-to-be-divorcée in part because I have two little children, tons of debt, an addict drug dealer (bad combo) for an almost ex-husband, and am the daughter of the patent holder of the "Super Tiger" and "Paper Tiger" (currently the most effective and NRC/DOT-approved transportation systems for low-level radioactive waste), a man also known for saying inspirational, reality-based remarks like "You better learn all those goddamned environmental laws or you'll be pouring coffee for a fat man."

Yet I also work for BDM because I have a significant background in public health and communications, have witnessed the creation of the 911 system in California, helped create a teratogen database for the UCSD medical school, and have interviewed a multitude of paramedics and firefighters to ascertain that the reason men were not putting oxygen masks on when entering a burning building in the 1970s was because their chiefs were not. I have learned about behavior, health, and certainly have seen my share of public health education initiatives, including the typical STD stuff on campus as well as the budding work on AIDS, which expanded vastly in the 1980s.

Fred jumps up and gives me an earnest handshake, offering me a chair, and I am unable to tell if it is my nerves or his that quicken the room and suddenly make everything brighter and clearer, vibrating the pulse of the fluorescent lights and making him slightly green—could that be the yellow paint?

I likely also occur to him as extraordinary: five foot ten and substantial, with green eyes, an angular face, and I'm Ken Gablin's daughter to boot. My father the entrepreneur holds nine active patents for specially designed containers capable of safely transporting certain types of radioactive waste. He filled my childhood with science, experimentation, risk, and the marriage of atheism and Catholicism. My dad has a reputation for being very direct, often polarizing people, and is both loved and despised in this industry. I never know by who or why at any given time. It is my very own version of the German physicist Heisenberg's uncertainty principle that the position and velocity of an object cannot both be measured exactly at the same time, even in theory. I am often in situations of uncertainty, yet at least I have been taught that uncertainty is universal.

I lower into the metal tilting chair with its vintage base of four wheels. The sound is deafening, amplifying my self-consciousness, and is louder still when I turn or lean forward or back, even a degree. I set my deep-plum bag down beside me on my right, straightening my skirt and settling in to listen.

"So I hear you're going to help us get out of this goddammed mess we're in with the EPA," Fred says with two parts relief and one part disgust, his hands landing on one of at least seven piles of papers clipped together, each pile twelve to fifteen inches high.

"Yes," I say, and smile deferentially. "As best as the team can." I am assuring both him and myself.

"Those tree-huggers need to get off our backs and out of our shorts, if you know what I mean. They don't have any goddammed experience or know-how to help us . . ."

I write notes about the various operations that are impacted by the lawsuits while Fred moves from paper pile to paper pile, naming the key points in each.

As I am taking this in from him as context, and sorting what it all means, something deep within me begins to cognate the full range of the sequenced 8 x 10 images I see on Fred's walls. One after another, at somewhat different angles or shapes or sizes, I see that they are all images of mushroom clouds. Some of Hiroshima and Nagasaki, and others of aboveground tests in undisclosed locations.

As I drift outside my own body, Fred's voice hums in the background of my crystallizing moment of horror, as if somehow a part of me tapped into the screaming of the atmosphere as it was ripped at an atomic level—sand becoming glass, flesh becoming shadow, and Almighty God crying somewhere, hands in the air, dismayed, at the misuse of free will. The images set off a chain reaction within me, a reeling of "How could they do this? Don't they know? This is evil. What are you going to do?"

My stomach turns in a quiet, private, likely invisible way, as I do not notice Fred noticing. I arrive partially back to the conversation, if that is what you could call it, although it is more of a broadcasting dump of the frustrations that Fred holds or carries for his whole department.

You see, the DOE was created to keep the management of nuclear weapons separate from the military—to have them at "arm's length" (no pun intended)—from the Department of Defense (DOD). So the DOD places an order with the DOE for the number of warheads it wants each year, and the DOE builds them. People working on these weapons need to have "Q" clearances or higher due to the nature of security, nonproliferation of fissile materials, etcetera, etcetera, etcetera. Even people like Fred that work with the leftovers of the process (radioactive waste) need clearances, because it is believed that spies and Cold War bad guys can work out what we are doing backwards from what we have coming out the back end. On the other hand, the Nuclear Regulatory Commission is in charge of civilian nuclear power plants—a completely different beast from nuclear weapons production. For me to become of any use to Fred as his hired hand and environmental policy analyst, I will need a "Q" clearance, and they don't come easy.

Crossing right leg over left, my calf rubbing against the grain of my pantyhose, the *zzzhh* of L'eggs on L'eggs, the creak of my chair pulling me to the present moment. "Well, it looks like you've done a good job pulling all the pieces together and getting the elements of all the lawsuits in one place," I half-heartedly validate him with disingenuous alignment. These guys must really be messing up the planet to have this much paper coming at them from every direction known to man. I'll be killing a forest getting this all copied and out for review.

Like any self-respecting twenty-something single mother working for next to nothing for people that pollute the Earth and irradiate humans and animals for experiment, I pick up my briefcase, shake Fred's hand goodbye, and promise to get back with him in three days with a strategy. I walk out of his office, up the elevator, out the door, and into my car, where I lean my head on the steering wheel and go numb.

. . .

I am living with my parents in their three-level McLean, Virginia, townhome, clearly interrupting the life of their dreams. I am twenty-six years old, working on a mail-order California divorce, mother of two sons, Surya now five and attending the gifted program at Churchill Elementary, and Chandra, one and a half, being cared for by my mother until I can afford daycare. I am an unspoken survivor of spousal abuse, yet at this time I do not have that language for it, and the sole defaulting debt holder of a $50K note to Sovran Bank that my parents co-signed to help Sunji and I start a gem-importing business, along with additional consumer and student loan debt.

What I do know is a numbing sensation. It is the dull ache of being underwater, swimming for the surface to take in air, only to be told again by Sunji that I am wrong. To be hit with words, hands, books, over and over, the process reshaping my playful, bright self from fuchsia to beige. Like a coral reef once a whole palette of color and life, bleached dead, I have become a surrendered star swimmer.

People who are experts in this area say there are many dimensions of abuse. Physical, emotional, and spiritual—each of these manifestations can also take the form of neglect. Sunji seems to know how to use all forms in secret combinations, keeping me in a constant state of wary and weary alertness to the bruises, condemnation, and negation of my very existence. People who are experts in addiction say it takes two to tango, so I clearly have not learned how to stop my part in that dance either. I wonder what the coral reef would tell us if she could speak.

Weekends for me are both wonderful and deeply sad. No friends and no discretionary money. I love spending time with the boys, though, and taking them out to the park behind the townhome in the mornings, singing to them, pushing swings, throwing balls, and playing on the seesaw. The spring we arrived in Virginia greeted the return of the locust. The din of their abbreviated and impassioned lives echoed through the day and night. Cicadas would literally drop dead from the sky as if they had a bug heart attack. Littering the playground sidewalks, Chandra would pick up the dead ones, toss them back into the air, and in his twenty-month-old transcendental wisdom declare, "Cicada all done," as the crunchy thud made it all too apparent that he was right.

Upon graduating from high school, my father told each of us at age eighteen (granted, I had the advantage as the second born to hear him say this over and over to my older sister), "You know what happens to baby eagles, don't you?" His eyebrows would be raised above the frames of his glasses, as he awaited rehearsed answers, yet we gave him the pleasure of responding to his own call, as he delighted in emphasizing the metaphor.

"They get puuuusshed out of the nest. They either fly or go spppppllllaaattttt!" Spoken with verve.

And now, almost a decade later, I sit in the park, crisscross applesauce, grass prickling into the back of my thighs through my cotton, Indian block print wrap skirt, tossing cicadas up into the air with Chandra, living welcomed yet unwelcome in my parents' home, with insurmountable debt.

Clearly, I have gone splat.

. . .

Looking out my bedroom window, sitting on the edge of the bed in the quiet of a weekend morning, I feel a warmth radiate from within my chest. I know I can no longer live with myself, driving to Maryland in judgment and blame about the state of the world and these men whom I work for. I am straddling unintegrated purposes. I want my life to be filled with love and contribution, and here I am working for law-avoiding baby killers. I am laboring for the very men that created, and in ways, worshipped, the atomic bomb. I revile their mushroom cloud images, the company men, and myself for being in a situation where I not only need the job but see no way up or out to become myself in any way, shape, or form. I feel I need to hide my sensitivities and "muscle up," "act like a man," and "hold my own." All of which means I cannot be me.

I have lost most of me, and I know all of me will die in the state of condemnation I am in. My father is seemingly blaming me for getting pregnant twice (true that) and having mixed-race children (true that), blaming my mother for watching Chandra when she could have been doing other things with him (true that), and blaming me for the money Sunji and I have defaulted on with our Sovran National Bank co-signed banknote that he has to repay (true that). Mom is blaming Dad for blaming me, and they are likely blaming each other for my failings, as I often see parents do. You get the picture.

I am blaming myself for not listening to my body when Sunji touched me and I knew I did not want to be with him; blaming myself for all the domino effects of ignoring those signals. I breathe in blame and breathe it out—a toxic atmosphere made up of many tiny particles and moments, like the flour of baker's lung or the asbestos of mesothelioma, except worse because instead of only breathing it in, I also breathe it out, exposing everyone around me.

Wisdom is a Being and can come to visit,
so do invite her.

This morning, Wisdom comes to sit beside me on the bed—warm, simple, and true—whispering to me, a young, confused, very educated, very busy, very lonely mother of two little children.

One moment I am suffering, and the next—*bam!*—I am understanding. With this sudden visit of Wisdom, I know in a flash the whole cycle of life, the picture of all the man-made toxins being created by the poisonous emotions of greed, hate, envy, and anger. I realize that if I continue to be in judgment and blame about the Freds of my world, I will only be spreading more of the same. I see that I can listen and discover the original intention of the Freds. Why do they do what they do? However unreconcilable it might seem, what is their underlying commitment? Looking through the glass bedroom window and down two stories into the dense vibrating green of the leaves, I see two coming together in depth, and with the light shining though the gently serrated edges, I know Fred's ultimate motive is not maniacal mass destruction. It is peace.

Like a dizzying darkness lifting, I feel the shift from judgment and blame to something new. Seeping into me, seeping deeply into the cracks where gladness and happiness had slipped out a moment earlier, is a new balm, finding and filling the gaping hatreds and tiny misgivings, forming a contained whole. The choice to connect with Fred from the deepest, clearest commitment I can discover gives *me* the freedom to listen to him without my stomach turning, to perform well at my role, to establish myself into the family of things called BEING THE SOLUTION. I had pitched my tent in the camp of contempt. I had been the carrier and propagator of the toxins, an innocent yet guilty assassin of my own potential joy. Now I see and am amazed. I could have made a choice to find another job, to work for an organization "more aligned with my values," which would have actually been a reaction. As I receive the help to transmute blame to understanding, I am able to enter choice, to enter with full heart the belly of the beast in a state of choice.

On Monday, walking through the pale yellow halls, I feel now like a secret agent of good. If I can make a choice to stop emitting toxic emotions, others can as well. I figure that atomic weapons in all their enormity are an extreme example of our condensed fear, and that this fear can indeed split the atom. I am not saying this is scientifically true, and I am not saying it isn't true. I do know that the creation of nuclear weapons has had a profound effect on the human race's relationship to its own creativity.

I do not have proof, yet I do know. It is as if we are afraid of ourselves, at war with ourselves for having committed an unforgivable crime, at a still point of marvel and horror. Many words have infiltrated our common vernacular from atomic weapons development, testing, and use: ground zero, fallout, bang for the buck, awesome, the nuclear family. These words are guiding us home, guiding us to a greater place of collective love and understanding, guiding us to take back and repair our place as co-creators, healing both the split atom and the brokenhearted.

Wisdom is teaching me that states of mind—especially fear, blame, shame, and judgment—are as toxic as radiation, benzene, and asbestos. No one is talking about emotions in this way in the late 1980s, yet my body knows it, and I can feel it, for it is whispered within.

I contemplate what other wonders and signs the innate intelligence of my body can sense and bring to language today in a way that the world needs now. How about you? What do you sense that you do not yet act on? How can we all learn to listen to the wisdom of our bodies in the moment? In Lightyear, we call this Strategic Instinct.

Strategic Instinct is one of your birthrights and is there to help you honor intuition, imagination, and creativity as your primary access to creating value in the world. It complements your analytical, knowledgeable mind and experiences. It is geometrically represented by an infinity symbol where the two hemispheres of your brain are intersecting back and forth in harmony—giving you the power that comes from having the picture in your mind match the language you have to describe and lead from.

What I sense and know is that

we are now entering an era of global leadership that is primarily led by the feminine aspects of intelligence, ending an era that has been led primarily by the masculine.

This means that both men and women are developing new skills, or perhaps uncovering ancient abilities that are based in Wisdom. I now know how to relate to values as Beings. With this understanding, what sorts of doors can we open and what does it entail? Well, it means you can invite Wisdom, Love, Grace, and more to the table to make important decisions and choices *and* require that mediocrity, guilt, obligation, greed, and shame find the exit door!

12

Become Your Own Hero

McLean, Virginia
Summer 1987

I am still in full "splat" mode recovery when I ask my boss, Katie, in the first week of work what I need to do to get a raise and she shares, "The maximum anyone can get in any performance review period is sixteen percent. I can set one for you as early as six months. You just need to get the site-specific radioactive and hazardous waste management plans from LANL, INEL, SNL, ANL, and Hanford, and analyze the Code of Federal Regulations (CFRs) for all NRC and EPA regulations that are indicated in any of the lawsuits DOE is facing from the NRDC, EDF, or the EPA. Then you should work with Germantown headquarters and write a draft internal order that will resolve the lawsuits and standardize the waste management plans across the country and in each of the different specific geologies, climates, and biological sensitivities where the new order will apply. Oh, and you'll have to get approved for a DOE 'Q' clearance to progress on this contract to do any real work."

Katie's voice is calm, as if she is sharing a shopping list to make layered eggplant parmesan. In another life, Katie could have been an excellent schoolteacher, for when I tilt my head quizzically, opening my eyes wider and smiling with playful, bewildered interest, she takes the look to mean *Break that down, please!*

"LANL is the Los Alamos National Engineering Laboratory near Los Alamos, New Mexico. It specializes in assimilating research and development solutions . . ."

My mind begins to muddle.

"And INEL is the Idaho National Engineering Laboratory . . ."

SNL, ANL, Hanford.

Her centering voice beaming monotone glaciers of acronyms, "and we'll help them clean up these sites for future generations, as the half-life of some of these radionuclides is 250,000 years." Her speech continues, and my mind spirals up and out into a geologic time frame beyond ordinary human existence to sense the enormity and immediacy of the task at hand.

The letters such as NTS and LANL scatter across my brain much like at Chandra's childcare center in my office park, where magnetic letters of the alphabet are scrambled at toddler eye level across multiple surfaces. Listening to Katie, I feel like a child savant. If I could step far enough away from the letters, I could perhaps decode them from the air, as done in the quasi-sci-fi *Nova* or Carl Sagan TV shows postulating ancient astronauts visiting the Earth.

Katie's list feels unreal, yet part of me says, "Sure, I'll do that."

Katie likes me. We are seemingly the only women for miles, aside from secretarial support in the BDM offices in McLean or in the DOE offices in Maryland. Katie is around forty and unmarried. She had a lover that went off to the Vietnam War and did not return. She never dates. She works. In that way, we are the same. My DIY divorce is bobbing along, floating in a stream of unattended paperwork some-where in the California court system.

Katie speaks to me in clear, unemotional terms about things like death, war, and weapons of mass destruction the way another woman might speak about nail polish, hair products, or retorts to pickup lines. All topics I have limited direct experience with; all of it surreal. Katie wears sensible shoes, drives a four-door sedan that is always clean, and eats her lunch brought from home at her desk every day. Yet I know there is nothing sensible about the world Katie and I are living in and attempting to transform from the inside out. There is a way that pain and trauma have been so normalized that our humanity can be lost in the business of living. Katie knows it too. She sees my youth and my energy, and she begins to mentor me through the dark halls within my own mind and sense of self-worth.

THE Q CLEARANCE INTERVIEW

Gathering in a small room in Germantown, lights off and the film reel rolling, we step back into time to watch a black-and-white secu-rity breach prevention short. Several of us "Beltway Bandits" need briefings; the moviegoing crowd is composed of myself and perhaps seven to ten middle-aged white men I don't know. The film characters are three late-twenty-something uniformed service men making their way around town one evening (location undisclosed) when they are approached by a heavily made-up Soviet woman with a strong accent.

"Hawhat ahr jew boys doing?" she asks.

The service men exchange glances.

The Beltway Bandits chortle.

"I kann tschow jew a rrreeeall goot time."

She leans towards one of the men, her bare arm rising above his shoulder, and places her palm against the wall of the building behind him. Close. Clearly a come-on. I grew up with Rocky and Bullwinkle and learned young about the Cold War cartoon archenemies Boris Badenov and his tall, sensual sidekick, Natasha. The guys at Jay Ward Productions must have watched this short for inspiration to create the Natasha character.

"Plenty friends for your friends. All goot gurls, ferry goot," she purrs.

The targeted man smiles, sending willing "yes" eyes to his buddies to gain alignment on the proposition.

The film's plot feels like it is taking a turn down the syphilis and gonorrhea paths of prevention, when the clear hero of the story whispers to the man against the wall, "George, what if she's a spy and wants our military intelligence?"

Wall man gives a knowing "Buddy, you just saved us all from committing an act of treason and possibly blowing the world up" nod. The servicemen, using their deep training for moments just like this to steer clear of Russian spy hussies, keep walking. Large block letters appear on the screen:

SAY NO TO WOMEN THAT APPROACH
YOU ON THE STREET

KEEP AMERICA'S SECRETS SAFE

ZIP YOUR LIPS

There's probably much more happening in this dynamic film, but I get the gist. I amble out of the screening room, my eyes adjusting to the lights. The guy that sat next to me mutters to himself, "Well, those were the good old days." I have no idea what he means. There are a lot of levels to be interpreted. I leave with the message that security is about not sleeping with sexy Soviet spies with accents like Natasha's. I am certain that I will not be a target of such tactics. What would that film look like? The camera follows me as I walk down a dark alley in a foreign country with two of my besties, tipsy from red wine. We get approached by a mustached, swarthy, seductive Soviet man aimed at peeling secrets out of me in my weakened state. *Hmmm . . . yeah right.*

. . .

A Q clearance application consists of many, *many* pages detailing each address where I have ever lived and each job or volunteer position I have ever applied for or held. Woolco Credit, Louisville, Kentucky, April 1974 to November 1975. Baskin-Robbins never did hire me, yet Hickory Farms of Ohio sure did. Oh, and I volunteered at the Louisville Planned Parenthood as a peer counselor as well as the Sheltered Workshop of Kentucky, where I assisted permanently disabled people in stuffing envelopes and sorting screws.

My application has been in for review for six months now.

On my desk this morning, I found a very official letter stating there are discrepancies in my application and an interview with the lead investigator has been scheduled.

I do not know if these interviews are commonplace. But in 1980s corporate/government business life, as a woman in my late twenties, I know I'm not supposed to talk about things. Not about the problems at the country's nuclear weapons facilities; not about what it feels like to say, "Yes, I can do that," and know that I have no idea; not about how the men drink coffee way too long when it is time to get reports in and I'm always the one to put on the hustle; not about the looks, remarks, and soundless sounds people make when they learn I am a single mother: "Oh, and of two? Really?" and then back-calculating as engineers of all disciplines love to do; not about Chandra, now two years old, banging his head from time to time on the wall; not about not having any friends to talk to about what I'm not supposed to talk about; not able to cry myself to sleep. Not about not.

It's a week later, and I've reported to the selected interview room, which has no windows. Three people are already in the room, seated at a lower-than-desk-level table, their knees slightly up as if all in a parent-teacher conference on child-sized chairs. One man holds a clipboard, one holds his hands on his lap, and a woman adjusts the dials and knobs of a large reel-to-reel recording device.

The air is stagnant and humid, the light dim with the now-familiar fluorescent buzz threading through the sound of tapping and swallowing. The tape reels look the size of ones used for film. The recorder has its own presence apart from the people—a fixture of the space, almost a main character. It is clearly not considered portable.

Hands-on-Lap Man looks at me and gestures with his right hand to an empty chair across the table, clearly meant for me. The recorder sits between us—all knowing—perhaps a survivor of the McCarthy era, a silent soldier of the Cold War gunning for retirement, yet still working diligently in the 1980s, perhaps in its own eighties.

Hands-on-Lap Man speaks. (I do not know his name or role, nor those of the other two in the room, only the process before us. They each no doubt have potentially dynamic lives of love and loss, making quiet or loud sounds as they approach orgasm, shopping the wide aisles of grocery stores, parking their cars inside the lines, packing lunches for children, dreaming of vacations in Florida, and pursuing mysterious or ordinary personal passions of woodworking or medieval architecture.)

My heart beats fast, fluttering, as I sit in my chair awaiting orders.

Clllllick. The reels begin to turn, my eyes tracing the rotation.

"This interview is being recorded," says Hands-on-Lap Man. "Everything you say must be the truth, the whole truth, and nothing but the truth or it will be considered perjury against the United States. You are being interviewed because there are markers in your past indicating you could be vulnerable to the enemy."

My mind returns to the imagined swarthy, mustached Soviet man trying to pick me up. Does Hands-on-Lap Man have any idea that I don't even have an evening babysitter for this secret-exchanging soirée since my mom is *so done* watching the boys when I get home from the office? Does he know I live with my parents in a suburb in northern Virginia? Does he know how unlikely the odds are of me having the time, energy, or anything that could possibly lead *me*, a twenty-seven-year-old junior analyst, to becoming a security risk?

"Do you understand?" he asks.

"Yes," I reply.

"State your full name, date, and location of birth for the record."

"Susanne Esther Gablin, July 17, 1960, Seattle, Washington, U.S.A."

We proceed to go through my application line by line, each address from birth. This takes what feels like hours. It is certainly no "greatest hits" list, my life dried down to facts of times and locations marching in a syncopated sequence from Seattle General Hospital to a double A-frame cabin on Vashon Island, then on to a red-brick home in Louisville before returning to the West Coast and the Revelle dorms at UCSD (pre-Sunji), to an active mental hospital for two weeks, to three weeks at sea on the sixty-foot Finnish Swan (yes, for even that period of time, I supplied the DOE with the names of the crew members so they could vouch that I was indeed there with them, going a few knots, tacking against the trade winds of the Pacific Ocean), to a few weeks in D.C. and New York, then back to a suburban rental in La Jolla, sought out and leased by my more conventional roommate, and then to another rental (cheaper, cooler, and closer to the ocean), to the summer in Sri Lanka and India (me on a President's Undergraduate Fellowship and Sunji on a hash-buying trip), to the Del Mar rental house where I began living with Sunji, to the year in Del Mar living with Mrs. Helen Moss, then ninety-four years old, where I became both pregnant and married somewhat secretly, to the miracle studio near the tracks on Twenty-Third Street where Surya was born, to McLean, Virginia (my parents' home), to attend summer session at Georgetown, then back to UCSD as a resident assistant for married-student housing at the Coast Apartments (9388 Apt F, where Chandra is born), to a rambling rental in Cardiff by the Sea where Surya has a near-death bike experience while moving us to the Encinitas rental and where I finally run out of money and ingenuity and return to my parents' home—to live, not visit, with my two little boys in full splat regalia—to now sitting in this room in this moment with Recorder Woman, Clipboard Man, and Hands-on-Lap Man, who looks up from his hands and his lap to gaze at me.

"Is this complete?" he asks:

My particle was tracked using multiple handwritten notes from my mother's address book chronicling all the places I have ever lived, patched with personal references, and typed up neatly on an electric typewriter without *any* white-out, as that would disqualify the application. Today, Google could have provided my interviewers with photos from Instagram and satellite images from space like those imagined by the genius Gene Roddenberry, creator of *Star Trek,* yet this was 1987, and while Reagan had begun the Star Wars initiative, we still worked with typewriters.

"Yes, sir," I reply. "It is complete."

Clipboard Man writes notes as Recorder Woman shifts in her chair, sensing the transition to a new section of something.

Is there more? Is that it? Are we done? How vulnerable could I possibly be to the enemy?

I became taller than my teachers by third grade, and yet now, even after two home births, I still have not grown fully into my own body, if that is even a possible thing. It was as if I was born a bat, wings folded in around me, shoulders like a collapsible umbrella tucked up nearer my neck than the anatomical norm.

I sense my smallness. The kid-sized chairs do not help.

Clipboard Man rearranges some of his papers and hands two sheets to Hands-on-Lap Man, who scans the first then flips to the second in rapid succession. He lays them both out on the space between himself and our massive icon of permanence: the recorder. One hand is on each paper, his palms down as if the wind could blow the sheets away, yet in the room there is no fan, no moving air other than that which is moving in and out of our nostrils. His hands take a stance, stabilizing, perhaps bracing, him for a climax of questions.

Hands-on-Lap Man peels his left palm up off the page, looks down at it, then to the recorder, and then to me.

"Are you aware of how much debt you have?"

I sense the heat of knowing the direction has changed.

"Yes," I reply. "About $54,000 of credit card debt and $30,000 of student loan debt."

"I see here your current salary is $23,000 annually."

"Yes, it is."

"How did you accumulate this much debt?"

The heat spreads from my face into my chest, a clutching swirl that both radiates and contracts. A rational explanation is needed where none exists, yet one must be manufactured. The silence and heat linger, and I sweat the chemical sweat that I will lovingly refer to in my lululemon talks twenty years down the road as the kind that can dissolve clothing, yet I am wearing polyester—the clothing staple of the 1980s—which only becomes wet. Within me there is no explanation—the debt just happened. It happened to me, a compounding of broken steps and unconscious moves that has had an external momentum of more, and more, in and in, down and down.

"I don't know," I say in a moment of synchronized truth. The kind of "I don't know" that speaks aloud from wonder, with an uplifting of the last word "know," an exhaling of fear and letting in of a new truth that I do not know cognitively, yet I could know, and in that knowing, I begin to speak.

Mindful that the three of them likely know more facts about my life than I do, I offer "Let me begin with the end, or at least the beginning of the end." This leaves me with the challenge to share what truth lies in the silent space between the notes of my life that are making the actual music.

"I am in the process of divorcing, in a slow, mail-order kind of way. You see, my soon-to-be-former husband doesn't even know I'm divorcing him, nor is he around to sign papers, discuss anything, never mind pay debt or provide child support. I began the process with the help of a friend and filed papers on my own, publishing my intent in the newspaper per California law when the spouse is unavailable." The ultimate do-it-yourself divorce.

Recorder Woman looks up at me and away from the recorder for the first time. Our eyes meet, and then she turns back to the recorder, tilting her head, her left ear turned and tuned towards me.

· · ·

There are moments in life and there are *moments* in life, and I have come to see that it is the faithful response in each small moment that leads to the big ones.

> *Responding to the daily call of love allows me*
> *to respond to the giant call of life.*

I have spent years reading mystic Christianity, meditating, attending devotional chanting circles, and knowing most of the words to many Hindu prayers, and after reading Bal Vikas stories to the boys, alongside classics such as *The Giving Tree*, I now have my own practice of picturing my future, forested and calm, far away from 1950s office buildings and the legacy issues of world wars. Yet I sense no shelter at this table. There is no walk in the woods to center myself, no inner song harmonizing my brain waves.

I have not yet discovered one clean and clear formula of relief or enlightenment. My life, as of yet, has not offered one answer. What there is, is a growing, loving trust of my own body as a receiver of help and insight through and with my sensations, and a growing trust of the vibrations that move me.

At the heart of everything is the human act of choice, of coming to grips with the total humanity of being in a body that experiences life through all the multidimensional senses—learning to cry or swallow; tasting; shivering; warm, skin-to-skin contact; the deep mammalian heartbeat. Learning not to cry. Unlearning not to cry.

And on this day, in front of my team of inquisitors, I express life by telling a story.

"It all happened very incrementally, sir. I mean . . . the debt," I reply to Hands-on-Lap Man. Out of respect for what I understand of their process so far, I ask, "Would you like me to break it down?"

If there is anything I have learned from Lincoln Logs in my own life or Legos in the lives of the boys, it is the value of components. Components provide insight, make a world of story possible, build a city, create history, and, to my mind, are completely underrated.

"Yes," Hands-on-Lap Man said. "Take your time, and remember, this is for the record."

I settle into my chair—a yielding, a surrender, a peace gathering around all four of us like a light snow quiets the sounds of the Earth, yet somehow punctuates the sounds of the sky, the surprising, emerging winter birdsong.

"You can see it took me a while to graduate from college, almost six years. Part of the reason for that is I had two children while in college, yet also I wanted to extend my tenure as the married-student housing resident advisor. I knew it would be difficult to pay market rent in the area where I lived, and as an RA, I was compensated with a two-bedroom home and $300 per month." My eyes are up, looking clockwise at Clipboard Man, Hands-on-Lap Man, and Recorder Woman to get a sense if this is the right amount of component pace. Clipboard Man, in his first gesture of note in what now has been over ninety minutes, nods ever so slightly in unspoken agreement.

It is not until much later that I put together his role.

What I do not say is that during those six years, in addition to sailing the Pacific and traveling to India and Sri Lanka via Korea, which all seem like plausible activities for a late seventies, early eighties undergrad, I took on many other tasks that came along with marrying the eldest son of eight children in a Catholic family that was part of the upper crust of Sinhalese society, a family that has all the tastes of luxury without the means to purchase it. In a matter of years, the formerly peaceful country of Sri Lanka initiated one of the bloodiest civil wars ever, consequently moving from the number-two spot for

literacy in all of Asia (second only to Japan) to right near the top of
the Amnesty International Urgent Action list.

Sunji and I found ways to sponsor his younger brothers one by one
and helped them get out of Colombo, the Sri Lankan capital. They in
turn would live with us, help with the kids, and sweep. I formed the
belief with much evidence that Sri Lankan men love to sweep.

"Suzy, may I sweep the kitchen for you?"

"Suzy, may I sweep the front porch?"

"Suzy, may I sweep where I just swept?"

I came to understand the sense of calm, control, purpose, and
contribution that sweeping provides. The contact of the bristles with
the linoleum, the certainty that the particles of living want to be gathered as a display of activity, leaning over to examine the contents like
soil scientists delighting in the discovery of a lost two-centimeter plastic part to the Lego train set, separating it from the true dirt. Back in
Sri Lanka, servants did the sweeping. Here in America, in California
no less, it was a grand adventure and a welcome task in a high-occu-
pancy, cramped, and servant-less space.

The man that is the father of my children, and my husband by
law, has no visible means of support other than me. There is the
occasional photography gig, or summer at the Boy Scout camp, or
slender profit selling hash, yet nothing steady or leading to a future.
"We"—I place quotation marks for truly I was lost—"decided"—I
place quotation marks for truly I was in reaction—to enroll Sunji in
the Gemological Institute of America in Santa Monica, California,
thereby giving him a career and a way to connect with his heritage. Sri
Lanka is one of the colored-gemstone capitals of the world, and surely
this step would secure a steady career. This, of course, meant owning
a car to drive to Los Angeles from La Jolla, the tuition of a private
vocational school, additional rent for his apartment there during the

week. All reasonable and worthy investments, but where would these funds come from? Credit cards, credit cards, and more credit cards. There must have been some rudimentary mailing algorithm timed to initiate 3.75 years after entry into university, and I was on *every* list.

CONGRATULATIONS, GRADUATE!
HERE IS YOUR CASH ADVANCE.

CONSOLIDATE STUDENT LOANS NOW!

Then a year later:

CONSOLIDATE
HIGH INTEREST PAYMENTS.

ROLL OVER HIGH BALANCES
AND EARN POINTS!

Another year later:

YOU HAVE EARNED A RAISE!

YOUR CREDIT LIMIT
HAS BEEN INCREASED!

Credit cards became the financial gateway drug to the illusion of prosperity and the reality of debt beyond recovery, debt that twisted what once had felt like the intelligent and resourceful part of myself into a sticky, tar-like heart of shame, its vibration pulsing low and amoeba-like.

I am not simply a person with debt. I am an indebted person. I am undeserving, a fool, a leftover.

"It began with taking a cash advance from my first credit card to buy a used car," I say, staid and reflectively, as if recalling evidence from a crime scene, yet still unclear if I am the detective, the victim, or the criminal.

"I paid the minimum balance for quite some time, and then received another offer in the mail to pay off the first one at a lower interest rate with a higher balance." Hands-on-Lap Man looks down at his papers, following the score.

"Student loan offers were also available, and I used those to pay tuition, books, and living expenses for the family to supplement what I was paid as the resident assistant. Student loan repayments did not start until after graduation." The recorder turns, providing consistent, omnipresent calm.

"By the time I graduated, I had several high credit card balances, multiple student loans, extended and immediate family members needing financial support, two small children, and a husband in school who'd started a gemological import business and used a lot of money but did not make any."

Clipboard Man is tracking along on his clipboard, making check marks with his pen as I speak. The recorder reels turn faithful and patiently, listening without bias, capturing the analog sounds of my voice.

Within me, an invisible band releases.

"You are interviewing me because of the amount I owe."

"Yes, Ms. Gablin." I am in a state of shock and thrill from three simultaneous sources. One: Recorder Woman has spoken for the first time. Two: she called me by what I only knew as my mother's name. And three: I understand.

"You see, we must investigate U.S. citizens applying for security clearances that are mathematically vulnerable to bribery." Her matter-of-factness is oddly soothing to me. She continues, "Based on your current income and likely expenses in raising a family on your own, it will take years, if not become impossible, to repay your debts. This is the type of profile we flag as vulnerable to bribery."

The thought of the swarthy, Russian mustache man now unwinds in my mind as the enemy. I see myself, the proverbial frog drifting to sleep in the warming waters of poor credit card and loan choices while the temperature rises, without alarm, even as the environment takes my little frog life while sleeping. Natasha Fatale came from a simpler world.

I nod, coming alive, batwing shoulders unfolding in a cellular knowledge of faith, knowledge of self being born, right here with the recorder turning, the most unbiased of all listeners. I remark, "That makes sense."

Clipboard Man looks at me, waiting.

Recorder Woman watches.

Hands-on-Lap Man, with hands on Ms. Gablin's credit report on the table, gives a small tilt of his chin up and to the left, his brows lifting.

In these days, I have not yet relearned to cry. There is a period of ten years that I do not cry. It is as if that whole spectrum of emotion has been set on "pause." In the absence of tears, as a release, my voice has retreated from its thespian-trained projection and vibrates with the small sound that comes when we touch the very edge of ourselves. The sound of approaching a barrier, or a prison, or an encasement. Perhaps the small sound a dolphin uses in short-range radar to know the shape of objects in its path and discover a way home. A voice of my own becoming in the smallest of steps perceivable—my own hero.

"I see," I say reflectively.

One thousand one, one thousand two, one thousand three, one thousand four, one thousand five; the amount of time needed at a stop sign in California to prevent getting a ticket when the Highway Patrol is watching. This is also the time that my body, mind, and spirit take to integrate choice, to act as the detective discovering my own innocence, while taking responsibility for crimes against myself.

Smiling fully, directing my swamp-green eyes (as my mom always called them), taking in the whole of the space, the whole of the moment, the whole of the situation, I tilt my head back ever so slightly, as if the sun could shine through the building and onto my cheeks.

"This is what I would want to know if I was in your situation," I say. "I am living with my parents now, and I direct my paycheck to food, daycare, and debt payments instead of housing. I purposefully took the credit card debt when writing up the mail-order divorce, as I knew my husband would default on everything if I left things up to him. Since all the debts and assets are held as 'community property,' I felt this was the best path. I learn quickly and will take the next position that has a higher salary. I have no intention of leaving things like this in my life by either filing bankruptcy or taking bribes."

Truth, a close cousin of Wisdom, has pulled up a child-sized chair beside me.

What I do not know to tell my interviewers, yet they likely sense, is that the same part of me that can keep a secret for my country for the correct reasons, can keep things secret for the incorrect reasons. I kept my own potential a secret from myself.

Truth, whether spoken out loud, or listened to within or without, has a sound, a vibration. At every level, there is a greater Truth. All people can sense Truth if they allow their body to be alert. In my work, I have found that humans are on a continual scan/sense/record protocol for truth. We want the way our body feels to match what is being said. When it does not, we know there is a lie, or we pretend or ignore. When we do not keep our own word to ourselves, we spiral into doubt and mistrust, and then see this in others.

As the inner gap between what we say and what we mean narrows, Truth materializes without effort.

> *Truth does not require moralistic perfection. It can light*
> *on the darkest of lives like a butterfly on the mudflats.*

I collapsed shame and debt with my identity, yet in the midst of Hands-on-Lap Man, Clipboard Man, Recorder Woman, the recorder, and our visitor, Truth, I emerge.

In this moment, does shame transmute into self-love? Yes. I have debt to pay, yet once shame is lifted by telling the facts, the power to do what is needed arises.

Do I walk out of the interview and step into a life alongside the babbling brook with apples weighing down branches, reaching out to me as gifts acknowledging my newfound love of self? No.

The recorder holds the information of every address, place of employment, dollar made, dollar spent, dollar saved, and dollar owed. I face my life on this afternoon. The facts, ma'am, nothing but the facts. And in the facing of the facts, shame shakes loose its grip on my future.

I am granted a "Q" clearance shortly after. I receive the maximum 16 percent raise and quickly leave for another company, where I help write up the reports and proceedings of Chernobyl, and then in another year to a smaller "Beltway Bandit" in Alexandria, where I learn everything about the mother of environmental laws, NEPA—the National Environmental Policy Act.

My boss, Katie, co-signs a consolidation loan for my debt by putting a certificate of deposit as collateral. Where? Why, of course at Sovran Bank, the very same bank where Sunji and I defaulted on the gemstone business loan to my parents. I repay the debt consolidation debt to Katie in three years.

I repay my dad posthumously and humorously in creative and playful ways such as buying a home for my mom in Santa Monica, taking her to China to walk the Great Wall and to Fairbanks, Alaska, to see the Northern Lights. I imagine if he were alive today (he passed in 2008), he would say the Sovran Bank loan ended up being an investment in my PhD of Transforming Failure into Success. That day, in the windowless room with the recorder, I began the journey of becoming my own hero. Of giving up the right to be a victim of my own choices.

I ask you, where can you put a star on your forehead and a cape on your shoulders and become your own hero? No more waiting, wishing, and wanting. Once you become a hero, your life becomes an action movie!

13

Win by Exiting the Game

We leave northern Virginia in the springtime, leaving behind the daffodils planted by Lady Bird Johnson in her day. The layered legacies of parks and gardens that grace Washington, D.C., are in full bloom as we wave goodbye to the moving truck that has packed our belongings. We fly to Denver to live in Boulder, Colorado, so that I may work in Golden, Colorado, the home of the Rocky Flats Nuclear Weapons Facility, affectionately known as "the bomb plant," where I have a role as an environmental policy analyst.

The house on Fourth Street, a one-story brick ranch with add-ons from each decade, rambles along the Boulder bike path. It has single-pane windows and eight apple trees in the yard. To the west is open space, brown hills dotted with pine trees and mule deer, rolling towards the Rockies. The remains of an old, abandoned stone house—the casualty of a long-ago fire—stand in the brush and invite curious children seeking adventure to enter and discover their own stories.

My first spring in Colorado was an enormous surprise. They say, "If you don't like the weather in Colorado, wait an hour." Temperatures can drop twenty degrees in minutes, and wind speed can spike enough to blow over cyclists. At the bomb plant, we are instructed to crack the windows in our parked cars to avoid having the windshields blown out from the air pressure changes.

Everything about moving to Colorado has been an adventure. The way the people dress, as if always prepared to go deer hunting, or hike a "fourteener"—as the mountains over 14,000 feet are called—or haul a truck out of the ditch. I've held a tight rein on the skirt suits, pumps, and L'eggs outfits of D.C., as my new role requires that I travel back and forth between the Capital and Rocky Flats every two to three weeks. I am considered an unofficial liaison, bridging the stark reality of shutting down a forty-year-old nuclear weapons plant with the theory and policy coming from the Department of Energy.

In the four years that I have been studying "those goddamned environmental laws," I have developed practical expertise, with NEPA in particular—the National Environmental Policy Act. It is, to my mind, the grandmother of environmental laws, and was enacted during the Nixon era. The law requires that if the government is doing something big—like building a dam or tearing down hundreds of thousands of square feet of radioactive, contaminated buildings—it needs to evaluate alternatives and look at the cumulative impact of whatever it is doing. Alternatives mean looking at what you want to do, looking at what you are already doing, which ironically is called the "No Action" alternative, coming up with some other ways to do what you want to do, and then comparing and contrasting all these options.

Cumulative impact means looking at the bigger picture. For instance, we need to look at impacts to the water, the air, the soil, plants, and animals. We have to examine health repercussions and benefits, yet also socioeconomics: Does the thing the government wants to do create or destroy jobs? What does that mean to the broader economy? The government also has to share its calculations in a large document called an EIS—or Environmental Impact Statement—through a series of public comment periods. It is not uncommon for these types of processes to take many years and cost millions of dollars, and to be political, adversarial, litigious, and tedious. I've essentially been hired for this adventure, of integrating and bridging polarities.

The boys are enrolled in Shining Mountain Waldorf School, and the Fourth Street house is a bike ride away in good weather. I meet all kinds of alternative and loving parents during our time here, and I suppose perhaps I am one of them. I love the colors of the classrooms, the way the teachers approach the children, the vast use of boiled wool, nature tables, large wax crayons, ombré-painted walls (before I even know about ombré), the parent-teacher meetings that include the "whole child." I love the way it feels to have the boys here; a dream, a goal of mine, has been achieved. I love the peace of feeling that they have a structure designed around them, crafted by Rudolf Steiner after World War I at the request of the heir to the Waldorf Astoria fortunes. A structure with a curriculum that so loves the human spirit, the very education itself can prevent further world wars. Or so that is the faith and belief during this time. I am also a believer. Shining Mountain is my way of protecting the boys from the life that I lived.

Driving each day out of the protected beauty of Boulder, I go south along Route 93 to "The Flats," the flat, barren territory that had been chosen in another war, the Cold War, to be the place to create the very special trigger used in modern nuclear weapons. The drive gives me time to free my mind of whole wheat, peanut butter sandwiches, permission slips, T-ball sign-ups, and the preponderant aftermath that is single parenting. Yet unfortunately, it is not fully single parenting. Single parenting is easy.

Sunji learned back in 1988 that the DIY divorce had come through, and he was in regular pursuit since then for reconciliation. He still shows up places, appears, sometimes with nothing, and he can persuade me through pity and poverty. Sometimes he appears with a wad of cash from some nefarious source, promising to pay me for all the back child support.

Today, as a sixty-year-old woman, I still have dreams of him appearing out of nowhere, needing something, begging, "Suuuusssee, please, darhhhaling," and I wake up, recalling the sensation of deep grief, like my heart is being ripped out of my chest, and I am still alive watching it being eaten.

Sunji came to "visit" with us when we moved out of my parents' to a house in Reston, Virginia. He came to "visit" when we rented a big farmhouse at Evans Inn, with its big full-moon swing hung from a huge tree, and he came to "visit" here in Boulder, once all the hard work of finding a home and settling the kids in class was done at our rambling Fourth Street house.

At this time, I do not see. Each visit is an extraction. He is away long enough that the natural resilience and love rebuild in my system, the light in my etheric body, the willpower in my bones, and the cash in my savings account. These build up enough for a "visit."

I have not professionally studied addictive or sociopathic patterns. Please exit stage right to find professional help if that is what you are looking for from me. What I do know is the gentle truth of having lived through it. There is a lot in these younger days that I do not know or see. The goodness of the realization that I am "food" in a pattern that I must end is that I can now ask God, "What do you want me to know and see today?" Dear Mother God and Father God, "What do you want me to know about your Kingdom and your will *today*? What do you want me to see and hear and act on *today*?"

These extractions from my ex-husband are sometimes short and sometimes drawn out. They always end when I am sucked dry of will and money.

It is painful to recall all of the complications that ensued. Suffice it to say, I am still quantumly entangled. I do not know I am becoming the cure. What we live through, we become the remedy for another. For instance, I say I am the homeopathic remedy for successful second marriages, for I have lived the whole scenario, except at this moment I am only halfway through . . .

It is a slow death. Which Greek god gets his heart eaten out every day by crows? Where is a teacher for this predicament? I am not even looking for help, because this particular death is so slow and regular that it mimics life.

I know enough to follow a thread of light to keep going. I am bright enough that I can work and deliver on my assignments and build a team and run a multimillion-dollar budget, yet I am so caught up in my own way that I cannot find my way.

. . .

Journeying from the theory and posturing of Washington, D.C., to the ground-zero realities of the military-industrial complex outside of Boulder, I learn to shift gears, zooming in and out, making practical decisions affecting lives of people I actually know. Such are the lessons of going from the big picture of the eagle to the detail of the mouse. Reconciling how the picture should look with how it actually is.

Connecting the lines in the *Highlights* magazine between the words and the pictures while I sit at the kids' dental appointment (yes, my job has dental insurance, praise God!), it dawns on me: The word "wife" is not matching with the picture I have of it from childhood. The word "husband," the word "family," the word "job." Vocabulary that is fundamental to my identity does not compute. Could this be the source of grief? My domestic life and role as "wife" has none of the playful, creative, intelligent tension of my parents' relationship, none of my father's provision. I have mimicked the loyalty, yet I am without the fundamental foundation of love and understanding that could allow a successful marriage to work.

Growing up on an island made me ridiculously resourceful. I learned how to shimmy down an eroding gravel and mud, 120-foot cliff to lay cable for our first color TV, how to flush toilets with seawater while resetting the prime on the pump for the well, how to return escaped Scottish Highlander cows that had "leaned" out of their electric fence, and how to use a public phone booth without any quarters so that it would just send the ring code to Mom. I was told by mentors that I was the sort that could "escape from a locked closet in shackles wrapped in a straitjacket." On Good Friday of 1987, my Grandmother Larson told me that Dear Abby was retiring and asked, "Have you thought to apply?" and "Why would you get a master's degree anyway in anything, as you already know more than most people?"

A background such as this, combined with the unexpected serial extractions of mind, will, and emotion, leads me to brew up schemes such as the following: When I finally, finally, finally (I think) get rid of Sunji, it makes sense to me to let go of my lease on the Fourth

Street house, save the rent money, and live in an abandoned teepee up Left Hand Canyon that is a half-mile hike from the road.

I picture picking the kids up from the friends who watch them after school, getting groceries, driving up the winding canyon, hiking in with the food, building the fire, doing homework, perhaps working on a craft, and watching them curl up to sleep. I would wake in the dawn, rekindle the fire, make breakfast, get the boys and myself dressed for a day at the Waldorf School and the bomb plant, and cruise back into town. I see myself raising boys to men, living back in nature, gathering wild onions, steaming the stinging nettles, and having an experience of a lifetime. With my lifelong gift of inventiveness, this option is incredibly appealing to me—and wonderfully adventurous.

Or I can get a roommate.

The latter prevails.

I put an ad in the *Boulder Daily Camera* under the "Rooms for Rent" section.

1BR IN 3BR HOME

with loving, responsible, single mother

$400

AVAILABLE NOW!

I have had roommates before. Many.

There was Patty, my assigned Revelle College colleague, who, on the first day of orientation, sized me up as a Southern, rule-following nerd and declared without hesitation or remorse that "You need a different roommate. I'm going to be selling, dealing, testing, tabbing, and dabbling with every drug known to man, and you and I can't be together." Before nightfall, Patty got herself moved over one room, and I was whisked to dinner at Marie Callender's by my new room-mate Jodi and her parents. I was grateful to Patty for her wisdom, insight, and effective room-swapping. Jodi gave me a new under-standing of the word "fan." She adorned our cinderblock walls with life-sized posters of Queen, and at age eighteen had been to every Los Angeles concert and knew every lyric to every song. Later that year, Jodi became a DJ. Patty became Wahila.

There are memories of Irene, whom the boys and I lived with for six months while Sunji got his gemological training, which flood my senses with the stinging scent and micro-trauma of Teflon pans melting onto the electric range—not once, but several times—giving me a lifetime dose of the sound of screaming Farsi and the smell of incinerated fesenjon, heating elements, and melted plastic pan handles. Privately, I called her "The Ireneian Crisis." As the months progressed, I shared my nickname for her with her, and she burst into belly laughs, probably smiling well into the next lifetime. When her lease was complete, she defended her failed fesenjon, faulting her "bad pans" and my "bad stove" as the culinary culprits. As a parting gift, she bought me a new "good" pan and hugged me deeply like a family member returned from the afterlife, her eyes moist. She likely only really wanted to make us a wonderful Persian dish, or perhaps share her own story, which in all the business of running a family, an apartment complex, and going to school, I never heard or asked to listen to.

Given my history with roommates, Patty (transitioning to Wahila—not sure why, but she just did), Jodi, and Irene, I picture that my next roommate will be a woman.

Yet no women answer my ad. In fact, only one person does.

Enter stage right—Charlie Hansen.

On a bold, blue-sky spring Saturday morning, as I arrive back home from baseball games with the boys, a VW hatchback from another era makes its way onto our dirt driveway. A slender, spry man emerges and walks directly to me as I stand on the back porch.

With shining blue eyes that see into new universes, the son of Cal Hansen—the head "mechanic" of the Livermore Electron Accelerator—Charlie beams brain waves with such intensity and brightness that some of his hair is gone. He thinks about everything so much and so deeply, I figure that is why some of the hair follicles can simply not survive the blast.

But I don't yet know this.

I yell out a greeting to this stranger, whose hand is extended as he approaches, cutting through space like the prow of a ship, connecting with me in direct and efficient form. "I'm Charlie. Let's take a look."

In his voicemail message, he shared that he wanted to live on Open Space, the beautiful land bought and protected from development by the City of Boulder, and on the bike path. The Fourth Street house has both, along with a great view of what was known as the "goat lady's" burnt stone home up the hill in back. The story goes that she was also burned when her house burned and that she wore a goatskin over her scarred face. Such are the stories of children, and hikes up the mountain, and double dare you.

He assesses the space of the long white one-story brick, single-pane-windowed ranch home with the eye of a geometrist. "You don't want me to rent that room from you," he argues, as if he and I have had any conversation other than "Hello, this is the hall, the bathroom, this is where I sleep, this is where the kids sleep."

I wait a beat, intrigued by his rapid and clear view. "What do I want then, pray tell?"

"You want to rent that room to me *and* the back room where I will set up my acoustic sound system and a sandbox to practice my tracking skills, and I will pay you $700 instead of $400 . . . Think about it. You don't even use this room, do you?"

Of course, I know that I don't have the money to buy any furniture, so it looks completely abandoned except for an old TV that Surya snuck in to watch on weekends. The back room is quite cold, as the landlords built it as an extension of the house. I am guessing there is little to no insulation in it. Frost often covers the outside and the inside of the windows. This is why we sleep in polar fleece and Chandra has chapped cheeks nine months out of the year.

Charlie has the energy and speed of a bird, and the patient intelligence of a lynx. Working in the places I have worked, I have met people numbed by routine and have also walked with geniuses. It is clear to me in my first minutes of being with Charlie that his mind is quick, powerful, and playful—and he *is* the only person that has responded to my ad!

"That *isn't* what I was thinking," I reply.

"I know," chirps Charlie, head cocked, smiling.

"It is a good idea, though."

"I know, that's why I said it."

And so begins my relationship with Charlie.

It is Charlie that gives the term "bomb plant" to the Rocky Flats Nuclear Weapons Facility. No one who actually works there, as I do, would ever dream to call it the "bomb plant." The focus and heaviness that comes with the work also comes with the full name. Charlie once leaned on the kitchen counter talking with a friend on the phone and said, "Yeah, I live with this girl that works at the bomb plant and her two kids . . . yeah, yeah, I know . . . wild, right?" I begin to see myself in the light of Charlie's view of me—kind, peculiar, special, and most important to me, part of me wild again like the star swimmer.

. . .

Charlie is in transition from partnering with a man named Neil on an acoustic company named Avalon where together they built high-end speakers. I've met Charlie at an enormous inflection point in his life, and I suppose I am in one too. We stay up late at night and talk about the best path to unwind the partnership and structure the financial and intellectual property. He becomes my first foray into what we would now call "coaching."

At this time in my career, I am managing the Rocky Flats Nuclear Weapons Facility Site Wide Environment Impact Statement Support Documents Project. Yes, people can and do have projects with titles that long that make sense only to the people working on them. I began the study of communications back in college and now have the opportunity to apply all that I have learned about "the medium is the message" and "the global village." These are both concepts brought to light by the futuristic communications theorist Marshall McLuhan. "The medium is the message" expresses the idea that if I communicate to you via radio, television, over the phone, or in person, that medium or method of communicating affects the message. Anonymously broadcasting via radio is not the same as sitting across the couch from someone.

The Global Village had to do with the rapid and localized connectivity happening across the world. We are now living fully in the world Marshall predicted. It is clear to me that for RFP to transform from an operating factory into a new version of itself, new ways of speaking and listening to the people working there, the neighboring community, the regulators, and government officials need to happen. I read about conflict resolution, attend workshops led by Quakers on the art of facilitation, and draw on my years of experience casting the *I Ching*—the Book of Change.

One of the most straightforward methods, at this point in time, to protect national security information is to segregate it. Meaning a person working in one of the buildings does not know what another person is doing. This way, the whole sequence is only in the minds of a very few people. The problem is, this information silo of secrecy creates a culture where the sharing of data, stories, ideas, and memories is considered a waste of time at the very least, to unpatriotic and potentially treasonous at most.

I have noticed that my mind works this same way, segregating the trauma of Sunji to grant me peace, albeit artificial, so that I can focus on the work in front of me. Silos in my mind separate home life from work life, membranes keeping the two in different holding tanks.

The Global Village is already pressing against the edges of Rocky Flats; organizations such as the Natural Resources Defense Council, the Environmental Defense Fund, and more are suing the DOE left and right to get information disclosed that has been withheld in the name of National Security.

One evening, many months after his move-in, Charlie and I have stayed up late. I am sitting crisscross applesauce on the couch, propped up against the couch arm facing Charlie, who sits smugly in the chair at the end. We begin "The Conversation."

By this time, I have listened to all the complaints and wrongdoings of his partner, the gaps in where the speaker design is and where it could be. It is common in these early days for Charlie to converse primarily about three things: whatever is "wrong" and how he can "fix" it, why people are stupid, and how I need to prepare for the End of Days when the sky will be red and the Children of the Earth will leave the cities to live in the forests. This last part of course works for me, as I have already calculated the move to the teepee up Left Hand Canyon for other reasons.

I can see my future, and I become the unspoken accomplice as I listen to Charlie, and although he feels better after talking things through, nothing really ever changes, and the same thoughts and feelings are there the next night. This of course gives me a sense of purpose, yet it is the lower-level fulfillment of catching the effluents of anger and disappointment, while doing nothing to transform any of it. Most people call this friendship. The future that is going to happen anyway is one of shared misanthropic dialogue and potential loneliness. And I can see it forming with the same certainty as ice does on a winter evening.

"Charlie, I have a game I'd like to play with you called 'meta-conversation.' This is an idea I've read about but have never put into practice, so why not experiment? The idea is that we have a conversation about the conversations we have. 'Meta,' as you know, means 'higher,' so it's like having a bird's-eye view, seeing things from above. You know how you love Tom Brown and his Nature Awareness and Tracker School?"

Tom Brown is a writer and teacher that Charlie has introduced me to that was trained by a Mescalero Apache and now runs a well-respected tracking school where he trains individuals.

"It's a bit like that where we look at things with some space and perspective," I continue. "From above, we can track the conversation and maybe see things we would not see otherwise. In?"

"In." He smiles.

"For instance, last night you said that Neil was a bonehead."

"That's right, he is."

"Okay, so here is Neil." I place a water glass definitively on the coffee table in front of me. "Now here is you." I place another glass next to Neil. "So, by definition, if Neil is a bonehead, what does that make you?"

"Charlie," he says.

Pointing to the "Charlie" glass, I say, "It makes you the partner of a bonehead, attempting to negotiate your way out of a relationship with a bonehead."

It will be years later that I will learn about the "essential reciprocity of being" from the works of Heschel. During the coffee table meta-conversation of simplicity, I only know that Charlie's future is stuck if he does not develop a new view of Neil. That once he has a new picture of his partner, it will give him a new Charlie. Or at least I can tell him to stop complaining about him! With every conversation, every thought, he builds a reality of being the victim of a bonehead. Nothing can work or move forward, as Charlie is too invested in being right about how wrong Neil is.

"I know I'm the partner of a bonehead. So what?"

"What is the future of a former partner of a bonehead? How well can the separation negotiations go for you? If who you are is right about his being stupid and wrong, then you will never find common ground."

I have grown tired of the circular, complaining pattern. I have become the roommate of a chronic complainer, forever and passively absorbing the complaints, so what does that make me? It makes me the powerless listener of blaming non-action—essentially an absorbent sponge but no more. The victim's accomplice. My power through condoning allows Charlie to be right and stuck about Neil being a bonehead.

Ha! I make a choice to love Charlie and instigate the ideas that could lead us both to higher ground.

Sharing self-development with others is self-serving.
Every friend and family member that learns self-leadership
tools becomes happier and stronger.

"Why did you partner with Neil in the first place? What essentially attracted you to him?" I ask these questions to discover a time when Charlie had a different relationship with Neil, one where he could respect some inner kernel of the man.

"Neil is an audiophile." Charlie chuckles. "And . . . ("And" is quickly becoming my favorite word.)

"What does that mean?"

"It means he loves music. He loves it enough and listens well enough to tell the difference of how components can change the sound. You know the cables in the sound room?"

I nod, picturing the enormous cables the size of a garden hose that lay dark, heavy, and thick on the worn beige carpet, unafraid and uncamouflaged, confident like a black rat snake curled up on the barn floor, owning its value in the ecosystem of the barn.

"Neil had me meet the guy that makes those cables. Those cables make the sound better. All of everything and how it is put together matters to the sound."

As was the case with Charlie, he begins to tell me all about the construction of the cables, the man who engineered them, why the length between the amp and the speakers affects the sound waves. He describes in detail the materials and how the point of connection is crucial. He reminisces about the inferior cables that he used before. I listen beyond when the average non-audiophile would have stopped and entered their own dreamland of internal dialogue, habitually smiling and nodding, prompting the speaker—who has long since lost their interest—to continue talking to alleviate them of the responsibility of actually being a partner in dialogue.

I stay with him. Listening. Belly on the ground, receiving vibration.

"Analog sound is completely different from digital. Digital sound ought to be illegal. As should Sweet'N Low." Charlie shares his factual insights as if he were reading them right from *Scientific American,* coupled with deep and unmitigated opinions (more on opinions to come).

Suffice it to say, as Charlie looks back at my face, large and angular in the artificial lighting of postgrad lamp options, he knows I have kept track and he has lost the scent. Perhaps he is trying to shake me off his trail, a trail that could lead to him owning responsibility in the way his own negotiation could be conducted.

"Whhhhaaaatttt?" Quizzical eyes, cocked chin, half smile on the left side. "Did I lose? Which glass am I again, and who are you?"

Tracking the conversation, listening for the bends and turns and branches that emerge from the original topic or question, is part of the skill of meta-conversation, yet the real insight is being able to perceive how we talk about how we talk. And so it goes that Charlie, my default roommate, nature tracker, and expert audiophile, teaches me a deeper level of listening and establishes my ethos that friends can coach each other.

. . .

Soon after Charlie moves in, on another late night, the kitchen phone rings. The boys are asleep, so I instinctually race to grab it and stop the ringing. In these days, phones have cords, sometimes answering machines, yet ours does not, and they plug into what are called "jacks"—little plastic connectors that link the phone to the phone company. It is a call I should not have taken.

"Suzy! What the hell are you d—" His voice is so loud I hold the phone away from my ear. Suranjith's ranting fills the kitchen and floods into the living room, loud enough for Charlie to hear as well— an unintentional speakerphone.

"You are going to pay!"

This is one of his favorite lines, and it has worked on me until now. Mostly, I imagine, because I have allowed a perpetual sense of being indebted to Suranjith for not completing some broken part of him.

"I never wanted a divorce! Why did you do it, Suzy? You are my wife!" There would always be a rattling and yelling following by something sweet like "You are the only one." At this time, I do not have the perspective to see that I am in a country and western song riding the story line of betrayal, sorrow, jealousy, and rage. "Cindi won't take care of me!"

Cindi is a kind, intelligent, and very wealthy single mother who has become the next person in Suranjith's lineup of soul extraction, and he is apparently calling me late at night to complain about his new girlfriend to his ex-wife.

People ask me now at Lightyear when I am working with them, "How did you start your career? How did you create this body of work? How do you know what to do?"

The only way to win the game is to not play it.

On this night, and many other nights before it, I am earning my own personal PhD of possibility, learning through trial and error how to be free, to be happy, to raise my sons well, to do big things like transform the culture of the U.S. military-industrial complex, and to do small things like stopping taking the bait. De-bait. Unhook from it.

"I am not going to talk to you about this," I say. "This issue is between you and Cindi and has nothing to do with me. I am saying goodbye now."

I ease the phone back in its cradle with Suranjith's voice fading as the earpiece nears its resting place, clicking on the clear plastic thingy that ends the call. The call is over, yet the effects are not. If I've learned anything during these years of working around radioactive materials, it is that the invisible matters. Like a song that gets stuck in the mind on repeat, I still hear his voice. It is a groove laid down deep in the vinyl of some unknown neural pathway, the phases jumping back to the same line; a glitch, a scratch in the album; a groundhog micro moment; the chemistry of this spiral caving my heart inward, my shoulders rounding. The structure of my being melts on the inside yet is whole from all outward appearances. This is one of the ways people die from radiation, and it is happening to me.

"Whoa . . . that was intense," Charlie says, walking into the kitchen. "What do you think he's going to do?"

I stand in the very place where Suranjith, the Christmas before, kicked me so hard in the back that I had blood in my urine. The memory is no longer a memory, but a reality returning. Touching the counter for stability and turning to my right in the darkness, I see the indoor hibiscus blooming in the greenhouse window near the dining table. What a miracle for this plant to survive here, 5,200 feet above sea level, protected by our single-pane kitchen windows, transforming water, soil, and light into such an array of tangerine orange petals. The silhouettes of blossoms as large as my hand are gray when backlit by the streetlamps outside, yet I know what color they really are, even in the dark. The memory of light. Some things are like that.

"I don't know what he will do and neither does he," I say, confident that I have said the right thing and done the right thing to end the conversation, yet then second-guess myself as all the previous fears surface in my tissue—the flinch, the recoil.

Time to sleep, yet not sleepy from the cortisol and adrenaline activated in my system, I turn to prepare for bed. The boys did not wake from the telephone, or if they did, they stayed in bed and went back to sleep before I check in on them. One of the most peaceful and beautiful sights in the world is a sleeping child. I re-tuck in my boys, whose eyelashes would make Maybelline models envious. Parenting allows us so many simple daily pleasures.

I take my turn in the bathroom brushing my teeth, seeing that Chandra's toothbrush is dry, letting me know after the fact that no tooth-brushing happened before bed. A pair of football pads lie on the bathroom floor. Chandra would sleep with them on if I let him. He is now six years old and in the Shining Mountain Waldorf kindergarten class. In Waldorf education at this time, students are not involved in team sports such as football or soccer. We play flag football and T-ball outside of school in various leagues and community groups.

Chandra is incredibly attached to his football pads, and with his frame thin as a rail, they rattle on his slender shoulders. The pads come in the car, into the grocery store, running errands, yet not to school. Chandra loves sports—all sports—and memorizes the names and numbers of all the players. With heavy crayon and marker strokes, he enjoys drawing himself and his brother Surya, large and in football gear. He can draw for an hour or more, seemingly always the same image yet with subtle differences of color, denoting different teams.

The Waldorf pedagogy advocates no electronics, television, and generally, no plastic toys. So, Chandra draws. Surya thinks. At age ten, Surya often tilts his head a degree or two to the left and is still for long periods of time. I have learned that these are not simply inactive mindless childhood blank-outs. I have learned to ask, "What are you seeing?"

"I am wondering if the rings of Pluto ever change. I am rotating the rings and looking at them," he has said.

Or,

"I am building a big house for all the coal miners, so they have a better place to live. I designed masks for them when they are working."

This is what Surya does while I fill out forms at the dentist's office and review documents for my work week ahead.

Here on the bathroom floor, the football pads have been laid to rest for the night to be picked up again in the morning. While living in McClean, Virginia, before the move out to Boulder, Chandra was given preliminary screens for early childhood development markers at his preschool. The head administrator recommended I take him to be thoroughly evaluated. This of course, meant more money and time, two things that a single mother does not have a lot of typically. My mother, before having my older sister Dory, had a career as a speech therapist. She urged me to wait and watch him instead of engaging in expensive and sometimes invasive testing. This was reassuring and gave me a path of least resistance. I hoped that the money I was paying for the wonderful northern Virginia preschool that he attended meant that the school had the resources to help Chandra. No. That was something outside their scope, and they urged me to work with a specialist.

Now here I am, two years later, looking in the mirror, brushing my teeth, football pads at my feet, doubts in my mind, and the shadowed, reverberating shouts from Suranjith's phone call forming a pit in my stomach.

I jerk my head towards the window at the sound of gravel giving way under a speeding car arriving outside—abrupt, unwanted, and impulsive. I brace myself when I hear the sound of a car door slamming and footsteps charging up the driveway, desperate and angry—the crunch of rocks, the echo off the foothills behind us, the sound of my mouth rinsing and spitting out the toothpaste.

Charlie opens the bathroom door without knocking, intuiting all that is unfolding.

"Would you like me to shoot him in the foot?" he asks with the same calm demeanor of "Could you hand me that pen?"

You've heard the saying "Don't shoot yourself in the foot," yes? That one refers to basic gun safety—don't accidentally shoot your foot with a loaded, cocked gun. The saying is now an idiom for unintended self-sabotage. "Oh, I shot myself in the foot, by telling him how I really felt!" or "You really shot yourself in the foot with that one!" Yet, in the state of Colorado, there is a "Wile E. Coyote" law left over from the mining days whereby it is legal to shoot someone entering your property, as long as it is only in the foot. These are obscure and rarely used suburb protection privileges, yet of course, an encyclopedic roommate like my Charlie knows all these laws and more.

His words stop everything for an instant. In the mirror, I see Charlie behind me, with his clear blue irises that reflect the objective and hyperrational mind behind them. His eyebrows are up—he looks quizzical yet calm.

I have known Suranjith since I was nineteen. Pregnant, then married, then another child, then divorced, and now at thirty-one, I remain directly in his line of sight despite all my efforts to move to new cities. His leased, cherry-red BMW still running, his footsteps near the back kitchen door, which is unlocked. In all these twelve years, this moment of tooth foam and football pads culminates with Charlie as the first person to witness what I have lived with all of this time *and* for me to witness him witnessing. The wholeness of the loop is completed. I see that I am seen. Not since the intake form at the San Diego Midwives have I been seen like this. Something is being born. I have been hiding my situation (or thought I was) from the boys, my parents, my co-workers. I've hidden it from myself.

I do not have a wise and worldly explanation for why I did hide. My situation likely fits into some pattern or syndrome, yet this is what I've experienced and not theory. As soon as I feel seen by another human being for the totality of who I am—the imperfect loving mother, the courageous, truth-telling worker, the irregular yet grateful gardener of indoor hibiscus, the maker of tuna casserole with potato chip topping, the young woman sharing wisdom of meta-conversations while still trapped herself in a spiral of abuse—a spell breaks for good.

Looking up into the mirror, a touch of white slurry around my mouth, I meet Charlie's eyes and say, "No. But thank you for offering." I do not have the ability to share all of what I have just told you to Charlie while he is alive. It is not until I begin writing this book that I recognize the connection.

Wiping my mouth, I walk to the kitchen door and meet Suranjith, who has already entered and is passing the washer and dryer and rounding to the sink. Instead of stopping him, I walk beside him Aikido-style, with cat-calm, smooth, measured movements.

"Let's go outside," I say. "The boys are sleeping."

He walks with me the seven steps in parallel as I open the French doors near my indoor hibiscus and we exit into the cool dry air, the BMW running throaty all the while, exhaust seeping from the tailpipe.

"You know you need to leave now, don't you?" I say this as a statement more than a question. With the bright stars shining above us, the car engine idling beside us, the boys sleeping within, Charlie, my acoustic engineering roommate, on watch, and the football pads waiting for the morning, Suranjith nods and enters the car, its door still open.

What intensity makes a person's whole nervous system become calm? At this time, I do not know—I just know that it does.

For both of us.

The game Sunji and I had been in was over the instant I stopped playing it. I thought I had to win the game, *in the game*, to exit it. That evening began the quantum untangling. I had coached Charlie to cease the game of creating himself as the hoping-to-be-former-partner-of-a-bonehead. He went on to create a whole new company with new partners. My ability to see him and his identity on his own, uncoupled from his former business partner, gave him freedom and choice from the game he had been in. Charlie seeing me, valuing me, offering to defend and protect me without drama, gave me freedom and choice to exit the game of trauma and drama.

Where could you be in a game not worth playing? Where are you getting hooked? Where can you use clear "non-action" as action to exit games? Allow yourself to use meta-conversations to observe the bigger picture of what is happening.

Observe, release, make a new choice.

14

Be in the Front Row of Unlearning

Boulder, Colorado
Spring 1992

My heavy briefcase brimming with narrow white view binders, I sit on the patio of the Boulderado Hotel, light filtering through bright green spring leaves. I am joining Dr. Samuel Richards, the communications mentor I have hired for my project "The Rocky Flats Site-Wide Environmental Impact Statement." The project has sponsored this training directly from my budget, under my leadership. Tomorrow will be the second round of training. The first one was considered successful, and now we have even more people from broader departments, deeper operational experience, and higher authority. My heart is pumping fast, not from the weight of the case, but from its contents and what the future holds. Meticulously three-hole-punched applications of scientists, analysts, plutonium building safety specialists, metal shapers, HVAC maintainers, and air sampling experts who will be participating in tomorrow's Communication Training speak to me from the briefcase. Their written responses to questions such as "What would you like to get from the course?"

"The opportunity to share what I know."

"Have my work mean something."

"A way to cohesively share data."

"A new job . . . my old one is gone, and I'm fifty and not able to retire."

The truth of their intentions, speaking in the form of their varied answers to the questions, claws at my heart as I know that no project has ever gathered a diverse group of Rocky Flats workers to talk together. One of the main strategies to protect sensitive or classified information (military secrets) is to segregate knowledge, either building by building or process by process, so that only a very few people could know the whole. This separation allows people to know their part and do it well, yet it is common practice to not know or ask what is happening in a neighboring building. In addition, Rocky Flats has a manufacturing mission, not a research and development mission, so people are not asked to innovate or collaborate. I know that for my team to successfully gather the best environmental data to determine a future for how to best close Rocky Flats, we need a new culture of open and integrated communication across the plant. People who have worked here for decades have lots of tacit knowledge, yet are suspicious about sharing their knowledge for fear of losing their jobs or worse, as now environmental violations can be tried in criminal court. Hiring Dr. Sam and allowing him to mentor me in shifting the culture of communication has been one of the hardest and best challenges of my career to date. No one is even considering this an issue, and I am out on the bleeding edge.

"Okay, Sam. Here are all the people and applications we need to look through. I want to make sure we are prepared for tomorrow. You know what's at stake," I say with the determined eyes of the person writing the checks, with skin in the game, as they say, the eyes of the person who has made a promise to the taxpayer to ask questions worth answering—the person who has contracted several million dollars to engineering firms and put them all on deadlines.

Dr. Sam understands all this and recognizes the courage I have, especially as a young woman, to consider that what Rocky Flats needs to accelerate its cleanup is a new culture, not just new technology. You see, at the end of the day *we* are the cleanup technology. How and what we communicate, how we stand for someone or something versus just idly complaining, gossiping, or impotently explaining why nothing can work—*that* is what makes new actions and futures happen.

People often ask me, "How did you start Lightyear? What coaching program did you study to build your career?" How do I tell them it began with the star swimmer, the moon landing, the bus burnings, the pouring of sherry, the exhale-pushing of birth, the truce with the recorder, the final ending of the Suzy and Sunji Games? Here I am across the table from the person I am relying on to show me how to ignite transformation, how to have people see their lives and opportunities differently. I have focused most of my life up until this point on my career, as my home life has been so rocky and flat.

Sam looks at me, head tilting, moving from my eyes to the menu and back.

"Chardonnay?"

I pull out one of the binders and place it on the table, flipping through the pages, astonished, delighted, and anguished by the responsibility of delivering value to these people tomorrow.

"See here, Sam—look at this one, and read what he wrote." I turn the binder so Sam can read, and he places his left hand on the book with kindness as if his palm can read, looks up at me from above his narrow rectangular readers, and asks, "I hear you are seeing someone."

Somewhat jarred, I smile sheepishly, thinking of Brett, return to the task at hand, and begin to flip to the next tab, yet Sam does not move his steady hand.

"Well?" he continues, inquisitive eyes flashing back the spring evening light.

"We need to focus first."

"Yeah, I know. That's why I'm asking you," he says.

"Look at these binders. There's so much work to do. This is the biggest thing we've ever done, and we need—"

"Susanne, who is he?" Sam asks.

I can't help myself and begin to giggle. I met Brett officially only a few months ago as a fellow student in a Communications and Management program. Charlie, my housemate, had invited Brett over to our place after a bike ride. He hung out with us for a while and played soccer with Chandra in the backyard. Everything about Brett seems so natural, happy, and helpful. Such an enormous contrast to my past.

"How long have you been dating him?"

"I—"

"Have you slept with him?"

And now I'm leaning back in my seat, sensing perhaps his question has gone too far. Sam is not conceptual and professorial in his approach to coaching me. Everything is very, very real and in the now. Sometimes *too* real and *too* personal, yet his directness is liberating once I let go of my defensiveness.

"Yes, yes, yes," and I begin to laugh and realize *this* is the conversation we're going to have, and that my white binders and plutonium soil chemists will have to wait.

Sam then asks me, "Does he have a good relationship with his father?"

I pause and consider his question and reflect on how much Brett loves his dad and spends time with him, traveling the world and having existential conversations.

"Absolutely. He has a great relationship with his dad."

"Well, where are you going to live? Your house or his house?"

Again, I burst into a chortle, feeling the afternoon light filtering onto my shoulders through the trees. "Uh, I guess my place?"

The third question lands without any preparation.

"Does he want a baby?"

A exhale escapes from me, complete with spittle. "Sam . . . I don't know." I already have two children, and having another in the middle of this huge career is a daunting thing. Sam then pushes a Boulderado Hotel beverage napkin across the table to me. He says, "Get out your pen, write down three things."

I scramble to find a pen in my purse and then wait, hand poised above the napkin, ready to write these commandments.

"One, let him know that he's 'the one.' Two, ask him which house he wants to live in. Three, find out if he wants to have a baby with you. And when you get those answers to those questions, you can call me tonight. *Then* we'll talk about tomorrow's training."

The sweat that dissolves nylon is dripping out of my armpits as I drive home to find Brett waiting for me.

I say, "Let's go for a walk."

He smiles back at me. "Sure." I notice the gap in his teeth, the shock of black hair, his kind eyes. This is the man who, every time I say, "I feel so uncomfortable about how fast our relationship is going," will grin and say, "That's great. That's wonderful."

Brett knows how to both acknowledge the tension of growth within me and make it fun, without ever making fun *of* me. From these early days with Brett, I learn how to help people respond to their discomfort with a smile, knowing that they're not actually feeling pain, but sensing a new tension—it's the learning of a new way and a signal to growth. Nowadays, we call it "Lightyear kind of fun."

Brett and I hike up the Salinas trail in the twilight. The stones are now glowing in the transition to moonlight, the bushes are wrestling with the sound of the wind, and the air is bringing the fresh scent of high Colorado-plateau plants.

The air itself is curative for my trembling. We come to a place where three stones are gathered on the earth. Maybe the size of each of our feet, and we go to stand on these three stones. I take the hotel beverage napkin gingerly from the pocket of my cute button-down jeans and open it up, as if I'm reading vows already, so that I can refer to the three simple questions without fail and keep my word to the mentor and coach who's guiding me through the transformation of the culture at a nuclear weapons facility. And apparently through the evolution of my love life too.

I raise my eyes to Brett's and say, "Look, I had this really intense conversation with Sam at dinner and I made him a promise. I have three questions that I need to ask you. And I'm very, very, very uncomfortable."

He smiles at me. "Oh, babe, that's very, very, very good."

"*You* are *the one.*"

There's a pause, thick like the night. It may have only been a second or two. Yet, being the vulnerable speaker, sharing before there's knowledge of reciprocation, is always the greatest act of faith. My words have tumbled in slow motion through the space, releasing any need for reciprocation. I own myself.

I gain upliftment from speaking the truth.

His smile continues. And then, instead of words coming back, he wraps his arms around me and holds me close. The wordless words of touch. I take it in. My body releases.

"Oh, there's another one," I say, pulling back. "I have another question, Brett. Are you ready?" Ever playful, ever delighted, ever ready. "Here it is. Whose house do you want to live in?"

I notice the pragmatic engineer, finance guy, leader, small business owner, founder of Wave Rave Snowboard products, kick in, and he sees, his eyes looking slightly up to the sky, head tilting back.

"Oh, well, of course. We should move into your house, and I'll rent out my place on Mapleton. And then I think we should get another roommate, when Charlie moves out, because that would be great for cash flow."

I realize that on some level, he's already been thinking about it but hasn't been expressing it to me.

Dear ladies that are listening: Men wait to be asked. They're far more complicated emotionally. Understand that. It's true.

"There is a third question."

I pause for only a moment. Brett is still smiling.

"Do you want to have a baby?"

The moonlight against his face. The stones under our feet. The gentle wind of Colorado sage.

"Of course."

• • •

October 1998

It is an ordinary Ramada Inn. The same one my old team from the Bomb Plant always came to for a beer after work in 1991. We lovingly called it the "RA-MA-DA" to make our adventure there and the dated 1970s decor seem exotic. Today, though, I am at the same un-remodeled building in a whole new life.

I am married to Brett, the mother of now four children, not just two, and a budding entrepreneur with a solid contract with a high-end communications and coaching firm. Brett and I have bought and sold three houses in our six years of marriage and are living on the "Hill"—the part of Boulder near the University of Colorado and Chautauqua Park. Brett has successfully sold his step-in snowboard boot company, served his one-year contract as the VP of Marketing, and is working alongside me at my communications firm while he trolls for his next entrepreneurial gig. I am experiencing a level of freedom, self-expression, and confidence that is unprecedented in my life so far.

How do I know that? Well, even with all the kids, laundry, shopping, homework, sports, and whatnot, I wake up and create my day. Ever since I started the Conrad Group in January 1993, I have been living in the creative gap of self-directed structure, and I love it. Right after I delivered my daughter, Hunter Anne, on October 22, 1993, I knew that I would not return to a corporate role and that it was time to start my own business. I had developed relationships with the best people to team with, and through lots of work (and even more moments of standing in the gap of "where will the next contract come from?") I began and have never looked back.

In my first large contract of any measure, with a newborn strapped in a Snugglie, I teamed with two engineering firms. It also helped that the Conrad Group was a woman-owned company, which government contract teams need to increase their odds of winning competitive contracts. I worked out the specialty of being "best in class" as a project communicator. What that actually meant was this: I did a lot of liaison work between engineering firms and the scientists I had met and worked with at Rocky Flats. I helped figure out who to talk to in order to get correct information so that the firms could begin studying the extent of the contamination and the array of options to mediate it. The culture of secrecy and not sharing information was still in the process of being unlearned, and I had both the gifts, reputation, and opportunity to accelerate that unlearning.

From there, the Conrad Group became known for building solid technical teams of just the right people that could get stuff done. The Conrad Group went on to work with other governmental organizations, corporations, and individuals, giving me new ground to learn how to support people who were stepping into innovation and possibility.

This was one of the gifts I received from growing up on the island, watching my father invent technical products, yet also later witnessing him facilitate meetings. In the early spring of 1979, he had brought me into the headquarters of the American Nuclear Energy Council to a meeting where industry experts watched the footage of the closed-circuit video recording that made it clear that one of the reactors at Three Mile Island Nuclear Power Station had experienced a partial core meltdown. Meanwhile, Dad had stayed calm, helpful, and intelligent. There is no lecture hall to replace this kind of experience.

Now, in 1998, I am also experiencing *being* loved by my husband. Each morning, whether there is a baby crawling under the covers, or a preteen looking for pocket cash before heading to school, or faxes in the home office to respond to, Brett turns to me, reliable as the sun rising, kisses me, and says, "I love you." This kind of everyday, consistent kindness builds a type of superpower within me—a reservoir of resourceful resilience—like a well I can draw on for my family and clients. The marriage I am in now helps me build my confidence, my faith in myself, and now, six years in, begins to seal the leaky roof of my soul. The number-one reason men and women give as their "why," when they come to study with me at Lightyear, is to increase their confidence in their intuition. What I let them know is that the word "confidence" literally means "with faith"; *con* for with and *fide* for faith. Increasing confidence, especially self-confidence, can often involve a lot of unlearning.

For those who have not experienced it, I can say

> *the only thing harder than being a single, working parent is being in a relationship with the wrong person.*

For this reason, many divorced parents stay single because the sheer relief of exiting the energy-sucking drama is so rewarding that the elation in being single blinds them to the possibility of a marriage that works. They have no picture. Only the picture of the old one. Yet the adventurous leap from single parent to marrying the correct person is nothing short of a miracle to be celebrated every day, and I now *know* my life is magic.

My current Conrad Group contract takes me to Corvallis, Oregon, to the headquarters of a large printer manufacturer at least once per month to provide team communication and executive coaching. A new voice of authority emerges from me as I successfully transit from being a sought-after technical program communications company to honing these skills into my own coaching methodology. I begin calling it the "Conrad Method" and play on what I am understanding that if confidence is "with faith," then Conrad is "with radness"! This makes me laugh. Also, in German, the word "Conrad" can mean "bold," so I add all that to the mix and figure I am here to help people have faith and ignite the bold radness that is already within them.

I work alongside other developmental professionals and produce a yearlong executive program that involves all the wild and woolly things you might expect, such as sleeping in yurts and keeping brown bears from eating the Mounds bars. More specifically, what I am truly hired to do is guide executives to see inauthentic patterns that block them from greater happiness and fulfillment.

In addition to the satisfaction I experience through being an entrepreneur, Brett and I have the means to take vacations. Brett is Canadian, so we travel there in the summers and sometimes to Mexico for family gatherings in the wintertime to get out of the snow. This is my life and I am grateful for it and enriched by it. Having a good life form out of a difficult one creates an interesting problem. On one hand, I am grateful to be out of debt and to be running a profitable and growing company, yet my success is tempered by deep fears of returning to loneliness and a low bank account. I feel the presence of the past, a shadowy silhouette of doom around the corner. I also feel the tension of staying the same while not wanting the other shoe to drop, so to speak. On the other hand, I want to learn more, be more, give more, and break into another level of contribution. I begin to see that enjoyment compounds and brings happiness not only to me, but to others.

I am at the Ramada to attend my first Dorothy Wood Espiau seminar. I had been invited by Merry, a local integrative healer who worked with my fourth child, CJ, right after his birth. With a background in craniosacral work and visceral manipulation, she came to visit him in his first weeks to check if he needed any adjustments. Often the forces at play on the skull of a baby as it is being born are very great, and there are those who are trained in how to gently adjust the components of the head and support the optimal circulation of cerebral spinal fluid. Merry said CJ was in great shape and then offered to work with Chandra, who at that time was ten years old and receiving all kinds of special support services for his loosely diagnosed cognitive disabilities.

Chandra had an IEP—an Individual Education Plan—meaning the public school had tested him and outlined the kind of support he needed in order to learn most effectively. It was difficult for Chandra to focus, to follow through, to read, to tell time, to do math, to make and keep friends, even to organize his backpack. Most of the things expected of ten-year-old boys were in the challenge zone for Chandra, and he did not get to experience daily success at school the way I had as a kid or the way his brother, Surya, did. I've spent many dollars and hours researching the brain, human development, and various methods for helping kids such as Chandra—approaches such as phoneme awareness, eye therapies, names of things that at the time of this writing I am unable to recall—and so when Merry offered to help, I said, "Yes! Please do!"

Merry and Chandra went into his room downstairs for forty minutes or so, then both emerged—Merry calm and professional, and Chandra bounding like Tigger in Winnie the Pooh. I thanked her for the home visit, and she left to visit the next family on her list.

Chandra darted into the kitchen to wash all the dirty dishes in the sink (the home we lived in at the time had no dishwasher). He washed them so well that we could actually eat off them (unusual for a ten-year-old, and unheard of for Chandra). Dear God in heaven! So many elements of this were absolutely new. The doing of a task that needed doing without being asked, the follow-through to complete the task, and the excellence of the task itself. Brett and I looked at each other with "what just happened?" eyes, but we didn't say anything for fear of breaking the spell.

I see Merry a few days later in her office and the conversation goes like this:

"What did you do in there? Chandra started washing the dishes right afterwards and it was amazing."

"Well," she begins, "I added information to his morphogenetic field for success."

Um. "Morpho what?" I ask.

Now mind you, my company works on environmental cleanup strategies for radionuclide contamination—stuff that can make you sick or, in high enough doses, kill you, and you can't see it, smell it, feel it, taste it, or touch it. You need a Geiger counter or similar methods to detect radioactivity. I am familiar with working in the realms of the invisible, yet her evaluation seems really out there, even for me.

Merry smiles. "I entered new information into his brain rings, codes that switch on the brain for learning and help him cross the corpus callosum in places where it has been blocked. I did something called a 'Miracle Integration.'"

"How did you enter codes into his brain?" I figure I'll pass on asking about the rings and the morphogenetic field for the moment.

Merry reaches shoulder height on the large shelf in her office and brings down a blue manual an inch-and-a-half thick with a black comb binding. She flips to some pages marked with handwritten sticky notes. Clearly this is a book she uses often. She opens to a page with steps written clearly, like a recipe with a box around the text. Below is depicted a small, outlined figure of a human body with an oval drawn around it. Numbers and instructions correspond with various specific body parts.

"See here . . ." she says, touching the page. "In this case, 'Circle R/C 4-7' means use your right hand and circle over this point . . .'" Merry indicates the place on the diagram that corresponds to the body. "And state 4-7." She flips through the manual. "This is filled with all kinds of codes for different things."

Merry smiles and continues. "These are the ones that helped Chandra." She points to the pages with "MIRACLE INTEGRATION" at the top in capital letters.

"Is this something you learned in your craniosacral studies or when you were learning visceral manipulation in France?" The depth and documentation of the work is evident to me by looking at the clarity and directness of both the visual and written instructions. I've been on the other side of the equation, having written many an environmental operations manual in my day, and I admire the structure and detail on the pages.

"No. This is completely different. Unrelated, really. There's nothing like it. Completely original." She touches the book with its scattered notes and tabs tenderly.

Of course. Just insert a few new codes. Easy peasy. "Well, it was a miracle to see him do those dishes!" I chuckle and then a thought occurs to me. "Merry, can I learn to do this? Can I do this on myself?" You see, I was raised in a world looking for proof of how and why something works, yet I know direct reality, like clean dishes, when I eat from them. As a mother of a child that is marginalized, challenging, and very dear, I *know* that I need to know, and to learn.

And so the intention is activated to learn this work, both for Chandra and for myself. A part of me wants to believe that things can be different for Chandra, different for the people in boardrooms and behind desks in cubicles that I coach, different for all the creatures great and small without voices spinning along on the planet, while another part of me rests in the need for practical proof. So, like Madame Curie, I set out to test things on myself. I set myself inside the great experiment that leads me to the aluminum exterior door handle of the seminar room at the RA-MA-DA.

. . .

It's been two years since I first met Merry, and I am just now able to fulfill my intention to meet her teacher—ultimately, the person who helped my son wash the dishes that afternoon in early June.

That's why we call them "in-tensions"; they are the
tensions within us that draw us forward from within.

I open the door and walk through, as we all must.

I sit in the front row.

The table I am sitting at is dressed in a white cloth skirt with a large white binder at each place setting, a pen beside the binder, much in the way I would set up a room for corporate trainings that I lead. Pitchers of ice water condensate, rolling into the silver platters underneath. Flowers at the front of the room and a large flip chart with markers. All unremarkable.

I am friends with the front rows, having chosen that post for my many 500-person-plus college courses, likely as a reaction to being forced to the back row of every grade school classroom due to my height. I now ask people to be in the front row of their own lives.

Being in the front row of your own life means that you lean in, learn and unlearn, that you cheer for your teacher because you care about yourself enough to make everyone's time valuable.

Your life matters, and at the end of the day,
we are our own teachers.

As a single mother paying for my own college classes, I understood that I was paying my professors, and we both had a deal to keep. To this day, when I lead in-person workshops, I greet the people in the front row, thank them, and let them know how important they are to the room. They set the tone and are part of the picture others see when watching the teacher.

There are twenty to thirty other people here, none of whom I know, save Merry, who invited me and encouraged me to attend. She beams at me from across the room, a hand-painted silk scarf with purple irises draped gracefully around her shoulders. She walks over to me, gives my hand a squeeze, and takes a seat next to me. You would think that with my zeal after Chandra's integration, I would have found myself at this seat earlier, yet lasting, substantial choice can be unpredictable, and mind you, my life is good, quite good, full and fast. A thousand other choices have displaced my intention. Perhaps this is familiar to you? Being of true contribution is always an interruption.

Her red hair coiffed to perfection, eyes both bright and commanding, Dorothy Wood Espiau enters the room, takes a black sharpie from the easel's shelf, spins to face us, pulls the cap off like a cork from a genie's bottle, and declares while writing on the paper as if all life on Earth depended on it—in paradox to the perfection of her hairdo—rapidly shaped cursive numerals:

"We have come to do five things!"

The tenor of her voice and the solidity of her tall stance in heels, tailored dress, and beautiful pendant make it clear she means business, and there is no question that the five things will get done. All without force, all with *power*. A radiant power that many call self-confidence.

Until this day, I have not met Dorothy or even researched her background. What I have learned indirectly is that her work has helped Merry tremendously with a closed head injury from a car accident, and that Merry in turn has been teaching and sharing integrations like the one she gave to Chandra two years ago—amazingly, the positive effects of that day still linger in our home.

I would go on to study for over twenty years with Dorothy, hearing stories of her childhood in Pomona, California, her marriage, her early career as a high-end wedding-cake caterer, her life-threatening health crisis, and ultimately, her dedication to the body of work she would create named Geotran. Till her last day—December 21, 2015—she never put a title of "what she did for a living" on her business cards. This would confound some and upset those who needed Dorothy to fit into a labeled box.

Her conviction funneling into her hands, relaxed yet strident, she draws the numbers out vertically, one below the other:

1.

2.

3.

4.

5.

Such are the advantages of the front row.

"Now, let's listen for what these five things are and get each one to 100 percent before Sunday at 4:21 p.m."

My mind begins a gentle, questioning swirl that leads to my own conjuring:

How does she know there are five things?

What does she have planned?

Am I going to learn a Miracle Integration?

Why are the five things blank?

100 percent of what?

Why 4:21? The course ends at 5:00, or at least that's what the flyer says.

The swirl becomes a vortex that I imagine I am containing with the habitual and studied self-control of any practiced student.

"Here." Dorothy stands in front of me and my front-row seat, her voice directive and gentle. She hands me a tin of opened, yet unused, perfectly sharpened colored pencils.

I come back from the swirl and stare up at her, curious and slightly stunned.

"Use them. It will make everything easier." One beat later, she adds, "For both of us." She chuckles, pauses, and opens her hand in a gesture of "Well, go ahead . . . why wait?"

Somehow free from the need to fight and be right, that everything must be explained first, then taught, and then summarized, I reach for the fuchsia pencil and take it in my hand, beginning the sketched outline of a human eye. Next, I highlight with a verdant green and spin a tendril out abstractly into a bird shape, and so it goes.

A remedy of relief and delight concocted from another, simpler time releases through my nervous system. I get it. I spend the next three days in the front row of my own life, drawing and listening. In another situation, I suppose I could have become embarrassed at Dorothy's gift of colored pencils and felt defensive or upset that my questions went unasked and I was told to draw, yet Dorothy's sheer clarity and love dissolves all of that. This marks the official beginning of my unlearning.

Although I am deeply grateful for the rigorous education I received through my years at the Annie Wright Seminary, Charles Wright Academy, Kentucky Country Day School, the University of

California San Diego, and for a class or two on Dose and Risk Assessment at Johns Hopkins, I've paid a high price for my knowledge. I've become over the years what I call "neck -up." A person who relates being right and having the answers with their identity. A person who overrides body sensations and instincts to conform and perform to the norm. A person who is smart and often prides themselves on being smarter than others, often as a way to hold power over them. Ah, the priciness of duality.

Through my education, I have learned to not trust myself and certainly not my body. I have learned to suppress my love for art, music, and dance in order to look and sound more "male," to stand out in a world of men and arm-wrestle my way through pay scales to make enough to afford to escape the doom of "low-income" subsidies. I have taught myself how to block feelings and compartmentalize them. I've learned to hate parts of myself, to compensate for living with this low level of self-hatred, and to become apathetic to my own deepest needs. Like the once-living star swimmer, the best of me has lived partially dead, encased in "shoulds," beliefs, invisible prejudices, and inherited legacies.

Mind you, to anyone else, my life now would be seen as amazing, and good . . . potentially even enlightened. I have gotten this far and have surpassed most of the odds weighted against single mothers for creating money and love. At thirty-eight, I am at a peak of my own creating. Oh, and I consider myself quite grown up and capable. And I am!

This is what I must shout at you from a place of love, dear reader, for you may not be able to see this for yourself. Many of you have wonderful and good lives and are unaware of the great within. You walk away from the practices of self-development believing you already have everything you need. We live tricked, and hence my dedication to being an interruption in your good life. The interruption comes with risks, though, and we all know this somehow, and

our fear of losing what is good blocks
the birthing of the great.

As we pace through my first ever "Gems of Excellence" course—the foundational one that Dorothy teaches—she methodically goes through all the bits and snags and glitches and micro traumas of learning—especially learning in school. Page by page, we write our names, the alphabet, composing in cursive, doing math problems. I experience a clearing of unseen stress that I never recognized existed, and yet when it is gone, I feel *great!*

For instance, as I draw out all the capital letters of the alphabet in cursive, I feel my body tense up towards the end and see a split-second memory where Mrs. Stone, my second-grade teacher, comes from behind me and over my shoulder, underlining my capital *Z* with a thick red marker as a way of marking it for improvement.

Other participants in the course share their various stresses and memories that come up for them in the group, and then together we learn to do Positive Points for Love Forgiveness and Choice. (The Positive Points are what I used on myself while waiting at the orthodontist when receiving the intense news from Surya.) We test again to see if the stress is still there, or if we need more identification of the worries or more Positive Points.

As if setting down a backpack I did not know I was wearing, I understand now the difference between good and great. I can *feel* the difference between being 98 percent and 100 percent. For me in the past, 98 percent was an "A+," so I had no context for understanding the state of wholeness that being 100 percent offered. With each exercise, I find that the releasing of these small, yet cumulatively enormous learning stressors has a rapid, beyond-talking-it-through-with-normal-language way of getting to the tiny invisible thorn of the past. I now have the memory of Mrs. Stone and her red pen, yet not the stress, not the deviously, ever-present sting each time I smell a pen, or see the color red, or feel a person behind me.

I began the daily habit of asking, "What is required for me to be 100 percent? How many things?" This simple, straightforward way of working was unheard of for me before meeting Dorothy, yet in my current life today, it seems as universal as Newton explaining the Law of Gravity. Gravity has always been here. And so the answers always have. It is having the correct questions that matter. For instance, if I only say, "Ten is the answer," there is no context for my listeners to understand the value of having the answer "Ten" since they do not have the question. If they know the question is "What is ten percent of one hundred?" then the answer has value. By asking, "What is required for me to be 100 percent" I get to: a. Know that I *can* be 100 percent, and b. Listen for how many things I might need.

After the workshop with Dorothy, I begin to unlearn more of my "neck-up" tendencies by continuing to practice the daily exercises she has outlined. I begin to learn to love myself, to love others, and to receive love. I begin to forgive myself, forgive others, and receive forgiveness. I begin to exercise choice on a whole new level. It is right at this time that I read Julia Cameron's *The Artist's Way,* a twelve-week, self-led course in creativity, yet for me it takes two years, as I have all these babies and moves and houses happening.

To paint a picture for you, in October 1998, Hunter is a fabulous five-year-old, wearing "Nala" dresses from *The Lion King,* with woolen Colorado girl tights and leather ankle snow boots. She is vibrant and deeply loved by her older brothers Surya and Chandra.

For people wondering about having a second set of children, I always tell them the older ones love it—the experience is a wonder beyond even a puppy!

Curtiss (we call him CJ) is two and a half, but rarely speaks, as Hunter is his advocate and personal translator. CJ's love of nature is already apparent, as a three-block walk to his preschool can involve twenty-seven minutes or more of careful observation of snails, slugs, birds, and stones. The little kids sleep (sort of) in their own rooms upstairs with Brett and me (they often climb into bed with us during the wee hours), and the older boys have rooms on the main floor off the kitchen. Chandra is thirteen and together we are stepping through the land mines of middle school and Special Ed. Meanwhile, Surya, now a driver at sixteen and a half, is a full adult whom I lean on often to help with *everything*. A shout-out to the eldest of any family, for better or for worse—we parents experiment on them by birth order. Suffice it to say, my day-to-day life is dynamic and more like a dance improv piece than anything.

Julia Cameron, author of *The Artist's Way*, has an exercise where you meet your future self and get advice. I do this and meet my eighty-year-old self. That Susanne simplifies things and lays it out like this to thirty-eight-year-old me:

"I see how much you enjoy studying the wisdom traditions of the world, yet do you also see how it can make you shallow and a master of none? You are here asking for guidance and I give it in the form of focus. Focus on one world religion and allow that to take you deeply in order to have access to all the others. Continue to study and teach the field of communication. Keep practicing Nia (a fusion of the dance arts, healing arts, and martial arts). When you are my age, you will be very happy you kept on dancing and singing! Focus on those three things as a foundation and everything will come."

This old and wise Susanne seems to really know what she is talking about, white hair and green eyes, sitting in a large camp rocking chair outside. I make a choice to study with Dorothy four to five times per year and learn what is not to be found in any book I can get at the library.

Second, I begin my commitment to create my own body of work to empower communication with oneself and others. Third, I become a black belt in Nia—and am still teaching to this day. I live from my core values of simplicity, wholeness, and artistry.

I am often asked, "Does this work last?" I always reply, "Yes, if you use it." Guess who I learned that from?

Dorothy.

Where can you put yourself smack-dab in the front row of your life? Can you become interested in what there may be to unlearn, perhaps even as a priority over learning more? I did not go looking for a teacher, and yet a teacher appeared. Perhaps one is right in *your* front row. For people to learn how to be happy, they often need to unlearn their generational and conditioned patterns of false drama, community through shared complaint, and the company of misery. Our brains are magnificent, *and* they will hold on to past pain and hurts to seemingly protect us from more hurt. It is our job to give the brain a break and unlearn the pity, the pain, and the panic. Through my studies with Dorothy and her work, I experienced that by restoring love, forgiveness, and choice to any life event or memory, I am able to unlearn the pain and recall who I truly am. So can you.

15

Say "No" to Good and "Yes" to Best!

Boulder, Colorado
Late Summer 2002

Zzzzhhh ZZZhhhhh ZZZhhhhh. The S-curve sound of a skateboard slaloming down 10th Street echoes in front of our house, the wheels whizzing over the chip-seal pavement. Though it is nighttime, it is still hot. The voices of college kids returning to the Hill, congregating on their front porches and drinking beer on outdoor sofas, waft through the open windows of our second-story master bedroom. Our "master" is really an upstairs living room with no door, and the breeze moves through the hall and out the back window above the stairs. This is our air-conditioning. Getting to sleep isn't easy.

Brett and I lie on top of the sheets, waiting for something to change that will allow us to fall asleep. Yet waiting on top of something, waiting for it to change, almost never works. We lay on top of the dreams we are pursuing that are going sideways in unexpected ways. We had left our traditional corporate coaching clients in 1999 to pursue our own new entrepreneurial adventure, inspired by the possibilities presenting themselves at the turn of the millennium—there certainly was no way to have predicted every obstacle that would be thrown our way.

That year, the dot-com reality was humming with opportunity. The world was both bursting with innovation and freaking out at the same time. Y2K was fast approaching. Bunkers with canned food and generators were being built in parts unknown all across the United States by people awaiting the Armageddon that would come with the changing of the millennium. Brett had made money in the market, which we began to use to finance our vision of a first-ever content group learning system, which we dubbed TwoJet. Users could create mini-courses, upload videos, set up a variety of permissions and roles—imagine YouTube mixed with Facebook and add the nonprofit educational organization Khan Academy—all before 2000. *Yikes.* We dreamed big.

Our company TwoJet was named for the simplicity of building webpages as easy as the Dr. Seuss rhymes of my early childhood books ("two" for collaboration and "jet" for speed):

One Fish
Two Fish
Red Fish
Blue Fish

One Jet
TwoJet

Red Jet

Blue Jet

Right off the bat, we landed a fantastic contract with American Crew, a men's grooming product brand run out of Denver, and began using our system to educate hairstylists and salon owners nationwide through our streaming, video-rich learning platform. Our clients could learn about new ways to cut hair, run their salons, and use new styling products. Both Brett and I are multi-tool players, and this would be our first time combining our skills officially—Brett in business structure and product design, and myself in communication skills and developing groups of people to run their lives and businesses in new and happier ways. *Easy! Done!*

Brett is a serial entrepreneur, having had success in his first two companies, Wave Rave Snowboards and Device Manufacturing, and building a portfolio in the market. We had no reason to suspect that we could fail. I brought the background of growing up in the home of an inventor, so financial ups and downs, the kitchen table calculation of risk, were as common as Frosted Flakes and Pop-Tarts. There were few limits on processed foods and sugars in my childhood. High and lows of blood sugar, the tides, and money were simply part of life.

I did not have enough suburban pull for normality to question whether we were spending more than we were bringing in, as chunks of investor money came in with regularity. Additionally, I was mostly through the "unlearning of being afraid to commit in a relationship" and was truly enjoying being married and building a family. There is grace and ease at every point of friction; in comparison to my first marriage, I no longer flinch at unexpected sounds or movements behind me. Three years ago, in 1999, Surya was thriving in high school, Chandra was getting great supplementary support in his learning journey, and Hunter and CJ were happy in their local preschool.

We'd bought a hand-hewn-log second home in the Rockies, took the kids to Baja, and returned to Colorado to the burst of the tech bubble in 2000. Still, our vision and contract steady, we continued to raise money for TwoJet and had significant local support.

Brett got all his news directly from business journals and the internet. We were a TV-free home, much as I had been raised. VHS movies were allowed, yet we did not have the news on in five rooms of the house as many families do, with a steady stream of controversy to take the place of conversation.

One Tuesday morning, in September 2001, I left to pick up Chandra at Boulder High School from his Special Education Immersion classroom to take him to a dentist appointment. I arrived at the school to see the world imploding. Before I had reached Chandra, I noticed that each classroom had their sets tuned to the aftermath of what we now call 9/11. Recognizing that the designers of this destruction used jet planes as missiles, I recalled working with my colleagues at Rocky Flats on analysis that examined this exact scenario, which we used to model for emergency-preparedness scenarios. The study postulated the question: "What is the dispersion of plutonium if a 747 crashes into the storage building?" Here, before my eyes, someone somewhere had the same idea and my concerns about a major breach in national security were high. The Pentagon was also targeted. We did not make it to the dentist that day.

TwoJet.

Two jets had crashed into the two World Trade Center towers. How completely ominous and ironic. We did not consider changing the name. Instead, we doubled our focus.

We continued with our work. It mattered even more, as the

technology allowed people to learn without the need to travel to large training events, considering air travel was mostly suspended for some time after the attacks of 9/11. We hired engineers and secured an office space.

September 11, compounded with the tech bubble burst, had investors in the United States skittish, and we borrowed money from my parents and Brett's dad against our better judgment. We were getting desperate, and still we continued on the path confidently, even as more money was going out than was coming in. Both our incomes were based on TwoJet, and Surya was now in college.

Here in the summer of 2002, we lie on top of this geology of living, the layers of it all, secret oil fields and undiscovered diamond mines, caves that lead to darkness, groundwater reserves from ancient times, the heat of the Earth and her beginnings, deep faults filling with magma, emerging to the surface. Lying on top of the sheets, sweltering in worry, I feel our "good" life shift.

Zzhhhh zzzzhhhh zhhhhh. Another skateboarder zooms down 10th Street, the sound bouncing up to our room, amplifying in my mind the unspoken stress of not knowing how to stop. A body in motion remains in motion. The momentum of TwoJet and the dream, careening downhill, means a crash is inevitable, yet if spoken, it means we will need to tell our investors their money is gone, a loss of reputation and possibility.

One of Brett's great attributes is stamina. He is a long-distance endurance athlete—a partaker in the Canadian Ironman and more. His ability to continue where others stop is amazing.

Yet stop we must. Interrupt, I must.

Yet I don't.

I can't.

I don't know how to.

All I know is to work harder, be more resourceful, be more sup-
portive, be more optimistic.

This is another way that being "out of choice" can look. It can
look very "good," very admirable, and yet it is very dangerous. In the
name of doing what I said I would do, in the name of being a committed entrepreneur, a committed wife, I am locked into one gear. I
have learned the importance of speaking my "no," of expressing my
"stop," and I have learned it through the challenge of not saying it.
Today, in Lightyear, I say,

Unless you can say "no," your "yes" is meaningless.

I am not sure how to tell this part of the story well. The heat of the
night air mixes with the weight of unresolved financial issues and the
invisible internal pressure to perform. Brett lies next to me, unable
to sleep, telling me his fears and then laying them on my heart. He
will soon fall into a deep sleep and I will lie paralyzed, processing his
words in the blackness.

"We may never get out of this," he says, flipping away from me to
his left side. "We could lose the house and everything."

I am silent.

"We have to get out of this." He flips to his back, speaking to the
ceiling fan.

I am silent.

"Do *you* have any ideas?" The emphasis on the "you" is spoken in
both retaliation and surrender to the late summer air's oppression.
Spoken to me and not to me. I attempt to throw off the blanket of
blame he has tossed onto my side of the bed, yet it still covers us both.

I deeply experience my own powerlessness at this point. I know
Brett is looking to me for answers, but if ideas do come, they will slip

out in these moments, which grate any wisdom I have left like the skateboarders' wheels on chip seal.

I develop a new skill. I begin to hear a very subtle grinding sound of Brett's mind, like gears and cogs not quite meshing, unable to compute, a dissonance. He has never failed. This is the beginning of his first failure. I, in contrast, have had many noteworthy failures. An out-of-wedlock pregnancy, a failed marriage, and a near bankruptcy after the mail-order divorce, to name a few. I have been able to say and act on the final "no" of my first marriage after I clearly saw what the cost would be if I, through non-action, were to teach my very young sons that treating a woman with violence and hatred was normal. Once the anti-vision became clear to me, the "no"—the "stop"—crystallized into focused action.

This situation is completely new.

I have a wonderful teacher, marriage, family, home, community, and investors, yet something deep as the magma far below me, high as the stars above me, both calls and eludes, creating unrelenting tension.

I am in the sleep-smothering discomfort of being at my own limits. I hear the micron-sized wavelength of violent blame in Brett's "*you.*" I absorb it as truth, and I witness my own familiar retreat into silence. Granted, his response is nothing like the five-alarm rages of Suranjith, yet the note left vibrating in the space between us foreshadows a future I do not want.

This microviolence is the 0.5 percent Dorothy was talking about. This is the 99.5 percent equals zero. Until now, her words have been a fascinating concept. In this moment, something within me tunes my awareness, slowing the beat down to the nanosecond. This tiny, disconnected bit, this snag in the sweater, this all-too-familiar turn of the downward spiral of self-brutality, will, if left uncleared, compound into human tragedy. It becomes the couples who fight, who divorce, or the couples who do not fight, who stay in the silent compromise of living together for the children, the settled-for reality of hearts closing so slowly no one notices. The men and women who never find love for fear of the micro violence that awaits all human communication, so they quietly tolerate loneliness and build compensatory activities to fill the void.

Sweat beads on my temples. Roxy, our one-year-old Doberman Shepherd Lab mix dog, is asleep on the floor next to my bed. I place my feet carefully to not wake her and sit up, looking out the side window, as if answers exist there.

This is the part I really don't know how to tell, yet here goes.

I give up.

I give up fully.

I 100 percent give up.

I give up my very "good" cognitive solution of finding ways. Soft and on the exhale, I say to myself, and to God, and to the night sky, "Help me."

"I am, Susanne," says an internal Morgan-Freeman-type voice, smiling at the humor of it all, as a cool Colorado wind shifts to enter our windows and lift the weighted air.

A new geometry of marriage begins to emerge over the next few weeks. I talk to God and God talks to me. Not in a priesty-Catholic-Churchy-Latin-Mass way (no offense, I simply want to share the distinction), but more in a let's-hang-out-and-sort-this-out-practical-yet-magical-friendly way. I invest the time and build my own relationship with God (please feel free to use the name or concept that you need to here. We have a whole Lightyear principle on discovering your inherited and choice-based beliefs around creation, yet for the purposes of this story, please keep reading) and have conversations. I commit to teaching Brett to do the same in his own way.

Then, and only then, no matter how many "take-twos" we need, Brett and I talk. About anything. Everything. Simple.

Different conversations begin to happen in this new geometry. For a while, Brett relies on me to get a clearer picture of what to do in our business, and yet sometimes he teases me for the way I work or do what I do, as I am sure this was very new to him and not a practice modeled by his parents in his childhood. I learn how to not take everything personally and how to stand my own ground and to have faith in a future without evidence. Brett learns to listen to his body beyond what he has experienced as an athlete and develops a greater sense of people and his own intuition. We take steps forward and backwards and up and down.

This can feel like no progress, yet as a student of self, I know this is my way of learning—the hovercraft art of listening and landing words. An adjustment here, an adjustment there. Sometimes the same words transform into different meanings. "I don't know," spoken from fear, shame, and distrust, becomes "I don't know," spoken from wonder, curiosity, and possibility. I take myself to the edge of my limits and let God take that very edge as a tool, carving me out of the star-swimmer resin.

Just as I have begun the daily practice of bringing myself to work, all of me—the integrated Susanne, the mother, the lover, the Earth steward and more—I begin the practice of listening *up* first. Listening up can take many forms, yet it involves the inner dialogue with God versus the outer comparison banter with the ordinary world and the unhelpful voices of mediocrity. It is the using of our sonar to bounce off the plans of Heaven for our direction, to listen for the best possible outcome, and to have faith in our role in its unfolding. There is no 100 percent solution in the ordinary back-and-forth of relationship communication—that much has become clear now that I know what

99.5 percent feels like—and even though I now dedicate my career to discovering and studying the best and most effective communication techniques of the time,

it is in getting the God communication set up that
"great" begins to make a home within my heart.

All of this takes about five years. Yes, I said that. Five years. Not ten days or "turn your world around in three weeks" or what have you. Five years. And that was to build the foundation of a great marriage, not just a good one. To this day, Brett and I practice a whole combination of things I learned from Dorothy: being 100 percent, listening *up,* and, most of all, catching ourselves when we are reactive and restoring ourselves to choice. That means noticing body sensations early and saying things such as "Will you forgive me?" "Let me do a take two," or "Can you help me get back to being myself and being in choice?"

In our foundational Lightyear Leadership program, Personal Legacy, each person creates an "insurance" plan where they tell at least three people close to them at least three different ways to help them shift back above the Line of Choice. Those ways can be a hug, a song, a photo, a word, a commitment, a walk, and more. Brett and I innovated the insurance plan those many years ago.

The short story is that, as we establish this new foundation of continual growth and greatness, we remain very happily married, we do not go bankrupt, and we eventually close TwoJet and move to Santa Monica to help open the first U.S. lululemon stores. I build more corporate-coaching clients using the communications background I have built. From 2005 to 2007, I serve on the board of lululemon, then transition to Director of Possibility. I begin co-creating great leadership programs by integrating and licensing Lightyear content to the progressive companies that align with empowering individuals with choice. Lululemon was one of them. Brett creates funds that invest in innovation and clean technology. We raise our children, generating the money for their educations in the nick of time! We then remodel our Santa Monica home a thousand times, travel the world sharing Lightyear, and discover how to hone our gifts as a couple. Too fun!

What can I accomplish if I listen *up* first every day and then do what I hear to do? What is possible if I bring myself to the front row of my own life, smile at myself, and cheer myself forward amid the missteps of life? These are the questions I still ask and practice daily. What becomes possible is a *great* life with wisdom and fun at the center. A world where you can become "the one" to fully live your life, knowing that your success will not take away from another's success—it will only add to it! The dog-eat-dog world of business, family, and community is nothing more than an old patriarchal paradigm rooted in fear-based struggle and competition.

People say, "Well, that is how the world is!"

"It is if you say so," I reply with a smile. How often we are unaware of the power of our words.

"I can't change it, so I just have to learn to live with it."

"If you say so."

Our words do not describe us. They create us.

In Lightyear, we begin with the principle "Everything After 'I Am' Creates."

Dog-eat-dog struggle is simply another inherited legacy to question and to unlearn.

Unless we interrupt the idea, though (or any belief, for that matter), we have no choice to change the direction of the program. So, to my students and clients, I offer the question "May I interrupt you and possibly contribute?" This often opens a door and I enter. "Could it be possible for things to be another way? Would you prefer to have your words build another world?" The train can, and does, take a different course.

. . .

People ask me, "Do you believe in God?"

I say "no."

I say, "I *know* God."

We hang out and chat. Not always in English. Sometimes in songs, spiderwebs with dew, signs on the side of eighteen-wheelers, and in the movement of the leaves. Great one to know.

Communion. Communication. Community.

These practices are easier and take less time and energy than holding on to petty resentments, waiting for the right time to retaliate, to prove a point, or to score a point in a game where everyone loses. When I fully understand and embrace these teachings of Dorothy's and incorporate them into my own life and principles, I find the 0.5 percent. I become a viral scan for my own life and can defeat the enemy within. She used to say the enemy is "in-a-me." The irony is, when you fully surrender and ask for help, you have all the power and control.

Part of surrendering and gaining 100 percent of your power is to interrupt the cycle of what we already know in favor of the unknown. The word "interrupt" means to cause or make a break in the continuity or uniformity of a course, process, or condition. It means to stop, to say no. A well-done interruption allows us to have a "take-two" opportunity for a new direction.

The heart of unlearning is becoming the interruption that contributes.

16

Generate Possibility from Self-Love

Vancouver, British Columbia
Leadership Conference
October 2007

My shoes are too tight. I have grown used to that, as I was born with bunions. They are my Grandmother Larson's bunions. The bony parts stick into the sides of my leather shoes as I walk in the drizzle to a conference room at the University of British Columbia, the moisture easing the leather. I like how these shoes look and have convinced myself they don't hurt. I have worn shoes that don't fit my feet my whole life and consider it normal, part of what there is to put up with—a "minor deformity," I was told by my doctor. Better than a major deformity, right?

Thankfully, the walk from the hotel to the conference room is short, and I am still on a high from my Nia class. This leadership conference has been consciously crafted to create lasting learning and community building experiences. For instance, at seven a.m. this morning, everyone had a choice of what kind of workout they would love to do to engage with other employees: running the seawall, taking yoga, doing weight training. I fancied that the most unique choice offered was the Nia class that I led featuring the music of Toni Childs. Nia, standing for Neuromuscular Integrated Action and translating to "movement with purpose" in Swahili, is one of the first forms of fusion fitness, combining martial arts, dance arts, and healing arts. It is artistic and cardiovascular. By this time, I am a Nia black belt. I choose to study and practice Nia in large part because it is done barefoot. No constraint, no bunions to crush in some inflexible ski boot or ice skate. The palms are the feet that walk the sky, and the feet the palms that touch the earth. All of that works well in Luon groove pants and a scoop-neck tank top. And while one could say the same of yoga, I found Nia years before leadership coaching found me. I fell in love with it and was already experimenting with its therapeutic applications.

Our group travels fast, chattering about how awkward they felt doing Nia, yet how free. A morning sweat always calms the nervous system, as we jack it back up armed with large lattes in our fists.

I am a featured speaker at the conference, and no amount of Nia can calm me. Even the caffeine is no match for the buzz in my body as it prepares to contribute.

I am in a new role now: coaching different company leaders and taking them—one-on-one—through the five conversations that later would become the Susanne Conrad Communication Series Level One: Personal Legacy. I work with CEOs, COOs, CFOs, Heads of Distribution, Training, Human Resources, Finance, Design, Merchandizing, Retail Operations, Community, and more, taking each one of them thoughtfully through this intimate and powerful process.

I began with what are now Lightyear classics: The Power of Knowing What You Want, The Line of Choice, I Am/You Are. As I began to integrate what I'd experienced as a girl on the beach, a teen in Kentucky, a single mother in university, a D.C. policy analyst, a wife to Brett with the opportunity for love, a communications and executive coach in corporate America, and a Nia instructor, I turned all my genius, flaws, and failures inside out. It was then that I found my ability to help others do the same increase exponentially. I was able to help people identify inner voices of fear and doubt that had held decades of grip, to see that these are *not the important voices* to listen to. Together we would laugh at these voices and call them silly names. This helps my clients laugh at what had previously gripped them.

Time spent with me was soon considered a gift by employees, quite literally. Radical as it seemed then, I was not there to goose performance or spy on weaker links. Each person was a human to serve and support in the unfolding of their greatest life. Period. Together we crafted personalized, everyday techniques for becoming mindfully aware in their lives.

I used everything that I had learned from Dorothy and could sense when people's brains were switched off from their goals due to some stress that needed to be cleared. I taught everything from how body sensations could become lead indicators to help employees become better communicators, to how each person could forgive themselves for past actions. I guided my eager students through ten-year visions and declarations to guide them moment to moment to happier and more fulfilled lives.

When I'd been asked to speak at this leadership conference, one topic and pattern became the clear standout to share: the positive power of Listening for Results. So many communications experts in my field focus energy on training and developing the speaking abilities of the leaders they serve, believing that leadership power comes mostly from what people say. What is not addressed is the ability for each of us to become our *own coach within*.

Consider this. We are always listening to the voices in our heads. If we begin to acknowledge our access to shifting, deleting, promoting, and firing these voices, we can have whole new possibilities. For instance, when I asked one of the women leads in a finance department what voice she had in her head that kept her from speaking up in meetings, she shared about her colleagues: "They will never listen to me." We broke it down so she could see that much like the early conversation with Charlie about his bonehead business partner, when she listened to that voice, she became someone surrounded by people who never listen to her. She had never taken the time to take the belief and turn it around in her hand to look at all the angles and underbelly of it.

Was she born with this voice? Where did she learn it? Could she unlearn it and even laugh at it? Was it even true? What new choice could she make? Her new choice was "I create space for them to contribute to me, and I have the courage to share." When she returned to finance meetings, she found herself more able to offer new ideas. You see, she had been in judgment of her team. Being in judgment is below the Line of Choice. Her judgment of them condemned her to become someone no one listened to. By being in discernment instead of judgment—listening to a new voice and a new choice—she then generated new possibility.

We enter the UBC campus, lattes still hot, and find our way to the conference room. It's underground and lit by fluorescent lights held in a high ceiling, the fold-up chairs fixed to the floor with flip-up, right-handed desks—a sure setup for many to be triggered with reminders of high school or college moments of stress and beyond. The space has capacity for several hundred, yet there are two-thirds of that in attendance.

Our group disperses to greet friends face to face, previously known only from regional product or community teleconferences. Some go to the washroom, to gather name tags, more coffee, to gather again, and find their way to folding seats. The mix of vibrant, solid block colors of tanks and jackets and pants, along with singing hearts, alights the space like a flock of tropical birds unstoppably expressing their morning joy.

My preparation for this moment has come naturally after months of coaching many leaders, their spoken and inner voices in my head. For today, I have written what I call a "flow"—a one-page breakdown of my intentions. I author who I am for these leaders. I design the logistics of their time with me. I architect the ideas they will experience and their order, how long it will take me to unfold each concept, and the time needed for each of them to share with the buddy beside them. Most importantly, the time for the whole room to share as a large group with individuals raising their hands, standing in their sometimes raw and sometimes playful insights. I know the tempo of the ninety minutes—its cadence, its song.

I call these preparations "flows" because flows are specific and rigorous, yet not rigid. They can be adjusted depending on what the group might need in the moment. Dorothy taught me to watch out for causes, dogmas, and agendas. Causes can suck out your passion, dogmas replace choice and intelligence, and agendas delete the ability to respond with inner hearing in the NOW to the larger need, for the sake of "sticking to the agenda" for sake's sake. Makes sense I would call them flows instead of agendas, yes?

It is time.

"For the next ninety minutes," I say, "we are going on an adventure as a community of leaders. We are transporting ourselves to a new set of possibilities, so arms and legs inside the vehicle," I say, teasing like the voice at Disneyland right before a ride takes off, cupping my hand over my mouth to imitate an outdoor announcer.

"Raise your hand if there's an empty seat beside you."

"Okay." I smile broadly. "You need a buddy beside you for the duration of the adventure."

"People in the back two rows, please stand up, get your stuff, and move to sit beside someone with their arm up." I sense the typical disbelief of moving the settlement, the enclave. One thing I have learned is that people get attached to their area and position in a space and often have little choice to change their habitual patterns of which they are mostly unaware. I've learned this leading Nia classes.

They rustle and begin the slow migration.

I channel my inner Jamaican bobsled team lead. "I know you be da back of da bus kids, yet dees folks up here are waving you up and dey *need* you." Mind you, my fake accents are all bad, and people that love and respect me tell me that I can shift from Russian to Irish to something off-planet unconsciously, and this is a distraction, yet it makes me smile. I envision my sister Dory bringing life to every inanimate stuffed animal, and for this reason, I am not embarrassed to use my variety of bad accents for the greater good.

"Come on doooown, the seat is right!" I say, Bob Barker-esque. Soft chuckles blossom in the hard light.

The back rows move, filling in all the empty spaces, like the turning of nutrients from the colder layer of the ocean to the sun-permeated surface, the mixing of primordial with present, the "wait in the back and see" souls perching into folding, fixed chairs right beside the keeners.

Thank you, God. As the next twelve seconds of movement happen, I hop down off stage to look into some of the eyes in the front row.

"Thank you for moving up!" I give a nod of alignment and scan the front row and beyond, now solid with color and willingness. I scamper back up the steps. Geometry established.

In an impulse from where I don't know, perhaps the morning Nia class I taught, I slip off my tight shoes and walk across the stage, pantomiming a woman in a flowing gown, allowing the wide, bell-bottomed backs of my pants to drag on the ground like a mini-bridal train.

"See that?" I turn towards them, then back and down at the pant hem, right hand gesturing to the fabric, pivoting to walk the other direction, left hand gesturing. "Do you see how long these pants are?"

Wiggling my left heel to shimmy the extra fabric, I turn fully to face them.

"These are size-12 tall *unhemmed*. I've been 5 foot 10 with this body type—these long, strong legs—since I was twelve years old, and not until now, at age forty-seven, have I gotten to have the feeling of this!" The feeling is the beyond-words sensation of *fit*. Fit in the broadest sense, a belonging, a well-being—a sense of being known and seen without shame or the need to shrink away. Fit as an expression of health, a standing taller and owning my space and body in a way I was unable to as a preteen. Fit in the sense of a quickening in the body where we have the experience of "yes." This. This is correct.

"God, I love this feeling!"

"You see, I am having an experience, a sensation, right now, that I had placed out of the realm of possibility when I was a kid. I remember at twelve, as a hormone-flooded preteen, searching for bell-bottom pants that were big enough and long enough. At the mall, I must have tried on every pair of pants. I could never find them, and then I stopped looking. I began to believe that what I was looking for didn't exist. And if the pants *did* exist, they did not exist for me. I did not know to ask or look again. At age twelve, I began to believe that stylish pants that fit *and* were long enough for me to *need to hem* were in the not-for-me folder."

Standing with palms open and fingertips streaming joy down the length of my legs towards my bare feet and beautiful pant bottoms, I sense the insight of generating possibility spread from the front row and ripple outwards.

"How many other things are in our lives like that? How many other things have we accidently or on purpose—through exhaustion, resignation, pain, or the closing of our minds and hearts—placed in the not-for-me folder, the not-possible-so-why-bother file?"

"Today we are going to take a deep look at listening, what we listen to, and how we can develop awareness of our listening, make a new choice, and produce new results in our lives."

I go on to tell them what I've also shared with hundreds of Lightyear clients: Be aware of what and who you're listening to, because not every voice is honest and true. These usually come from inherited legacies or negative events in your past, and it's important to identify which are truly yours and which come from somewhere or someone else.

Here are some examples of voices you may be listening to that don't have your best interest at heart.

The voice says: You're so shy.

You say: I won't go to that party because I'm shy.

The reality: You actually like meeting new people.

. . .

The voice says: You're too much for them. They won't understand you!

You say: I'll just keep my mouth shut because my ideas are too out there.

The reality: Your thoughts are innovative, creative, and important to share.

. . .

Or the voice says: You don't know what you're doing.

You say: I'll let someone else take the lead on a project because I don't know what I'm doing.

The reality: You are competent and capable of leading a project successfully.

Could it be possible that you learned these voices from what other people have said about you or to you? Maybe your father always got on your case for having wrinkles on your shirt, and now there's a voice in your head telling you to iron your clothes. Your voices may have more complex origins, but it's important to identify them so you can begin to choose what and who you want to listen to.

Once you begin to recognize the five main causes of reaction in your own body (worry, doubt, unforgiveness, fear, and judgment), you will start to notice the individual tones of their voices in your head. Learn to recognize both and you will be able to make a more authentic choice.

One way people combat these voices is by naming them. Perhaps one is a grumpy old man who is negative about everything, maybe one is a snotty teenage girl who is constantly judging you, maybe one is actually your mom! By identifying and naming each voice (Uncle Frank, Felicia, or just Mom), you can say "Bye, Felicia" when they start annoying you.

A "listening shift" is the choice to catch automatic, reactive forms of listening and shift to creative, choice-based listening that will provide the results we want.

I explain all of this to a rapt audience, and seventy-seven minutes of tears and laughter later, as I land my first of many conference workshops to come, I receive a standing ovation. I am jarred at first, resist a reflex to run, and challenge myself to allow it in. I feel my shoulders release the silent training of decades of deflecting appreciation as a passive nod to an overvalued inherited legacy of false humility. I say goodbye to my grandparents' voices in my head that say, "Don't show off or disagree!" or "Women are meant to work at home." My father's reminders to "Develop a marketable skill, goddammit" when I was busy pursuing an "impractical" degree in the liberal arts. I shift and choose to carry forward the dedication, courage, and intelligence of the generations before me, and step up and into a new state of freedom. I own the power of listening and the intelligence of my body. By receiving the applause, I honor the new choices of everyone that is participating.

I once attended a talk by Dr. Walter Alvarez, a professor in the Earth and Planetary Science Department at the University of California, Berkeley. He is most widely known for the theory that dinosaurs were killed by an asteroid impact. In the lecture, he essentially calculated the statistical chances that any one of us would be here on planet Earth as a human being. The odds were tiny! Like SUPER tiny. And at the end, with a kind and wise demeanor, he asked each of us to turn to the person next to us in the lecture hall and congratulate them on the excellent work of getting here, of having a human life, of having language to express ourselves. I felt so radically amazed!

It is time to "Get There Now." To give yourself a standing ovation for every chipped, cracked, failed, minor deformity and peeled part of your life that seems to not fit. Take every bit of it in your hands and choose it. Use the white-hot heat of transmutational self-love, allowing it all to pass away. Give yourself this moment in time and space to appreciate the radical amazing possibility that you are!

17

Get There Now

January 2017

The brain is magnificent. So profoundly designed, so divinely orchestrated, that we don't understand all of it. Yet your brain will reveal its majesty if you prompt it with the right questions. Your brain will show you the way home. It will allow you—as it did for me—to "Get There Now."

For decades, I've been profitably working with companies to develop their executives and leaders in my curriculum, yet I know I need more to really make the long-lasting, sustainable impact I've seen in my vision. Since 2005, when I wrote my first complete set of visions and goals, I've had this goal: "My complete curriculum runs on a sophisticated technological platform by July 2011." Well, of course, I am six years past my "by-when," yet the picture remains in my heart.

The spirit of TwoJet is still with me as well—the dream to join the empowering stories of a community of practice and to bring people together from around the world, teaching and learning from and with each other. TwoJet was a galvanizing experience in my emotional and spirit life, yet it has also left a trace of fear, or best said, I've allowed a trace of fear to remain uncleared. I know that the idea of Lightyear is the one to carry on the great social experiment of liberating people from mediocrity and apathy, *and* that it can be done! The importance of people taking the time to author their ten-year visions and compose a set of health, career, and personal goals to support that vision—and be able to share those goals and put them on the table of life like their cards in a great game of three-deck gin rummy—*that* is the next level of the great social experiment.

After facing and conquering my personal roadblocks—from an abusive ex-husband to near-bankruptcy—I have finally realized, after many, *many* years, that I have the power to change my life, and thereby the lives of others. Regardless of what happens around me, to me, and in my relationships, I can make active choices to create a new future, one that I might never have thought possible.

I can do this *now*. And so can you.

After I launch Lightyear, the concept of "Get There Now" becomes an integral part of the program. Everyone is always working to get from here to there in life over a long trajectory. But instead, why not get there now? Instead of reaching your goals after a lifetime, struggling through life's many hurdles as they occur, visualize yourself in that future *now*. What do you need to be there *now*? How can you bypass the barriers that often hold people back?

Our magnificent brains can help us achieve your new future as you want it to be. Through simple reeducation, we can create a new pathway in the brain to chart a new future. It's quite simple to begin to re-create your reality. It starts with changing perspective.

At Lightyear, we begin the "Get There Now" process with a

specifically sequenced inquiry in order to make your future a reality *now*. When I speak with a client, I begin with two basic questions. You can—and should—ask the following of yourself.

1. What would you like to change?
2. What would you like to be different?

The person I'm working with answers as such:

1. I would like _____ to change.
2. I would like _____ to be different.

When doing this exercise, always make sure to ask questions going backwards from the future as if the successful change and difference has already happened.

Once you've established what you want to change and what you would like to be different, in the affirmative, in the future, answer the following questions:

1. What is your future self doing?
2. What is your future self saying?
3. Once the change has been enacted, what are you receiving then that you cannot receive now?
4. What are you allowing that you are not allowing now?
5. What do you know in the future that you don't know now?
6. What door are you closing that you're not able to close now?

7. How many new choices are there to make?

8. How many new decisions are there to make?

Next, you must ask how many decisions and choices you *do* require to support that new life/future.

1. I decide X, Y, and Z.

2. I choose X, Y, and Z.

The questions lead you to a statement that we call the bottom line. When you land the statement 100 percent, you sense a quickening in your body; a "yes!" a "that's it," and an "aha."

The bottom-line statement is your true "Get There Now" statement. When you realize your statement, you'll sense a moment of "Oh, that's it!" It will be something brand new, essential, and very simple. This statement will give you a road map to getting to your future *now.*

Here's an example of how to find your "Get There Now" statement, based on a conversation I had with a client named Jana, an executive leader at a non-profit.

Susanne: "What do you want to change, what do you want to be different?"

Jana: "To work in a space where I feel the freedom to create without the incongruity of the team around me. I feel secure in my space."

Susanne: "Once this reality *is* changed and *is* different, and you work in a space where you feel the freedom to create without the incongruity of the team around you, feeling secure in your space, what are you doing then that you are not able to do now?"

Jana: "I am able to expand the impact of the work we do. I partner with more organizations and build a company that is focused on a unified vision for why we exist. I am crafting the communication and giving direction of who and why we are here. The team is rowing in the same direction and I am able to set the pace."

Susanne: "The reality that is changed and is different is that you work in a space where you feel the freedom to create without the incongruity of the team around you, and you feel secure in your space. You're able to expand the impact of the work you do. You partner with more organizations and build a company that is focused on a unified vision for why it exists. You're crafting the communication and giving direction of who you are and why you are here. Your team is rowing in the same direction and you are able to set the pace. Once you're doing all that, what escape hatch are you closing then, that you are not able to close now?"

Jana: "I am closing the escape hatch of doubt. I am closing the back-door of 'I am not the One.'"

Susanne: "Once you close the escape hatch of doubt and the back door of 'I am not the One,' what are you accomplishing then, which you are not able to accomplish now?"

Jana: "Helping thousands of people get out of homelessness. I am providing for my family more effectively. I am valued and compensated accordingly. I am saving money. And here is the big one . . . I am able to enjoy life, have fun, *and* make a difference!"

Susanne: "Yes, Jana! That's it. You can feel that in your body, yes?"

Jana: "Wow, yes! Absolutely!"

Susanne: "Now, how many new choices and decisions do you need to make to support this 'Get There Now' statement of 'I am able to enjoy life, have fun, and make a difference'?"

Jana: Mmmm . . . my choices are that

1. I choose to be the One.
2. I choose to stay in reach of the people I am here to help, learn from, and serve.

My decision is that

1. I decide it is okay to *want* to be the One.

Jana went on to implement these choices and decisions by having a greater sense of well-being while working through challenging issues. She realized that she needed some fun to help with the heavy lifting of her inspiring work. Jana also benefited from verbalizing her commitment to her community and team.

• • •

Being able to know the power of the now may be the only power there is. I have learned to err on the side of contributing in the moment and own the risk of being an unwelcome interruption.

"Get There Now" is a process I distilled with permission, alignment, and inspiration from Dorothy Wood Espiau. It does not replace her powerful work from "The Gems of Excellence," which I also teach to my Lightyear coaches in training. What this method provides quickly is a successful, future-based mindset. The familiar Einstein quote "We cannot solve our problems with the same thinking we used when we created them" applies here. "Get There Now" gives us the mindset to allow us to become the solution now. It works with the Lightyear principles of "The Body Is Innately Intelligent" and "Everything After 'I Am' Creates" by giving the person the experience to speak their choice-based future out loud and feel it viscerally in their body—what we call the "quickening."

Dorothy's strong voice of love, her unedited truth telling, and her capacity to use wisdom helped to cut off the soul-snaring brambles that block pathways to a more integrated and purposeful life. In one fell swoop, she could help me make a minor shift in perspective. She called those insights "just a little change" and helped me get out the chainsaw to chop through the "dead trees"—sometimes a whole forest, in my brain.

"Get There Now" is also a loving play on words and soulful salute to Ram Dass, the author of *Be Here Now*. I met Ram Dass a few weeks after Brett and I helped open that first U.S. lululemon store in the summer of 2003. He was being hosted in a small, beautiful home in Beverly Hills. This was after his stroke and he could not speak. I took my turn and approached him to say "I love you" and "thank you for all your work" and "I'm so happy to meet you in person" and "gosh, I have read all your books" and "I am so glad my husband has read all your books because that makes him a better person and helps him have a way to talk about God without talking about God because he didn't grow up with God yet he knows about the eternal and the essential as he studied your lectures and read Wayne Dyer in college and I am so grateful and oh, you are so funny and I love that about you and thank you for not dying as we all still need you here."

Of course, none of that run-on-sentence swirl of cosmic-fan gushing devotion is what actually came out of my mouth. I said, "Hi," and in that instant all I had hoped to communicate was communicated and more, and I felt a floating, fulfilled relief of being fully self-expressed, known, seen, and loved. Ram Dass did not have much speech at that point in his recovery. Yet communicate he did without speaking! Oh my goodness! He smiled at me right between the eyes and I felt a deep resounding love that still vibrates within me. So Ram, I trust you find my title funny. You probably knew way back then that I would be the one to write it.

Ha! First, Be Here Now, then Get There Now.

All power and access to everything exists in the Now.

What time is it, you ask? Now.

What time will it be? Now.

What time was it? Now.

Knowing this makes every moment new, possible, and sacred.

A book is like a long poem. There is no way for me to convey all that I wish to convey to you in the ordinary recounting of history, yet I can find the slender and supple willow branches that can weave a useful basket to repay you for your time and attention. My life is still unfolding, and yet it is time to conclude this particular work.

My wonderful, creative sister, Dory, died in 2008 at the age of forty-nine. Her death certificate said heart failure, yet that was likely an effect from morbid obesity. Her death was truly heartbreaking, especially for my parents, as it always is when children proceed their mothers and fathers. I made a habit of calling them every day after going back home to Santa Monica after her service.

"Hi, Dad, how you doing?"

"Hey, Slug. I'm doing *great*! Goddammit. Goddammit. That service you put together for Dory was great. Loved it. Want one just like it."

Dory's service had consisted of a small circle of family at the funeral home. We played "Somewhere over the Rainbow" and "Turn! Turn! Turn!" by the Byrds and talked about Jesus and heaven and had an open mic about what we loved and appreciated about Dory.

"I'm glad you liked it, Dad."

The next day, he called me.

"Hey, Slug."

"Hi, Dad, how you doing?"

"GREAT! Goddamn that service for Dory was great. Loved it. I want one just like it."

Mom had told me that Dad was suffering micro strokes and that his memory and cognitive function might be affected. So, as he repeated himself, I took that into account and replied,

"I'm glad you liked it, Dad."

Next day:

"Hey, Slug."

"Hi, Dad, how you doing?"

"GREAT! Goddammit. Goddammit. Goddammit, Suzy, that service you put together for Dory was great. I just loved it. Everything."

"Everything?" I asked. "Even the songs and the Jesus and immortal life part? I thought you were the kinda guy who responds to 'Hey, Dad, what happens when you die?' with 'You go in a hole in the ground and rot.'"

Dad chuckled, recalling our conversations on the Vashon ferry about life and death.

"Yeah, everything! Goddammit, I loved it."

At this point, I figured it was best to shift gears and fully take in his acknowledgment of me—his appreciation for Dory's service—because perhaps that was why he was repeating himself so much.

"I am so happy you liked it, Dad."

"Yeah, kiddo, now I know what you do for a living!"

"Ha, I guess so. Songs, a little dancing, some listening, some positive talking."

"I want one just like it."

"Okay, Daddy-o, you got it!"

We laughed and said goodbye.

The following day, I saw a call coming in from my mom while I was sitting in my call chair in my home office. I was on the other line with a young woman, Parker, whom I was training to be a Lightyear coach. Parker knew about my sister's death, and I hopped off the call to answer my mom.

I click over and hear my mother's voice. "Suzy, your father has died."

In that moment, I knew my dad had been placing a "service order" with me and was 100 percent coherent in his appreciation and request. Forever living and dying with a touch of humor.

With great gratitude, I share some of the essential, yet not limited to, learnings from people in my life:

Dad taught me to communicate, make requests, and be an entrepreneur.

Mom taught me to love beauty, design, order, and preparation.

Dory taught me how to be a secret agent, use silly accents, and unlock mysteries.

Brandy taught me that rescuing begins with sniffing.

Mrs. Moss taught me how to celebrate living and make avocado ice cream.

Melba taught me to watch for and become a miracle.

Suranjith taught me how to live outside the box by breaking it.

Celia taught me to release old pictures and trust my body.

Veronica taught me how to love without conditions.

Her mom taught me the importance of pillows.

Liz, well, you know what Liz taught us all.

Surya taught me how to be courageous and wise beyond my years.

Chandra taught me how to learn with new eyes and ears (and what off-sides means).

Charlie taught me how to become a great coach by being a friend.

Sam taught me that transformation anywhere is transformation everywhere.

Brett taught me to become lovable again and unlearn trauma.

Hunter taught me to sing, dance, and begin again.

Curtiss (formerly known as CJ) taught me to swallow life whole.

Chip taught me to love people by thanking them with opportunity.

Dorothy Wood Espiau taught me to teach choice.

And now *I* teach. Well, I don't exactly teach in the way most are accustomed to.

I teach tuning.

I have learned that I radiate a specific environment and vibration that helps people and organizations recall who they truly already are and *can* become. As they learn to read their records of truth and light within, they can also unlearn incorrect beliefs, patterns, and pictures. I have developed over five complete years of curriculum that I have been in the process of building for the greater good for over thirty years. I now do this through the Lightyear coach training programs, which are for people that want to liberate their transformative greatness and bring it to their own lives, families, neighborhoods, companies, countries, and world. Each level of Lightyear coach training focuses on a set of principles and concepts that, like Lego pieces, can be played with and arranged to create an infinite variety of wonderful courses. Each level radiates out from our personal responsibility and decisions to our social, corporate, environmental, and energy-related responsibilities.

Level One is called "Personal Power and Wholeness." There are nine principles in this level, and you have already heard about a few of them: "The Line of Choice," "Everything After 'I Am' Creates," and "The Body Is Innately Intelligent," to name a few. The foundational course that Level One Lightyear coaches learn to deliver is called "Personal Legacy." This course helps people identify inherited beliefs and release them and gives them the skills and techniques to write their ten-year vision and goals. On Lightyear.co, members craft profiles of their chosen future, write their vision and goals, and share them with the community—think of LinkedIn, yet instead of describing your past qualifications, you share who you are *becoming*. So fun! Anyone can take "Personal Legacy," and many people review the course every year or more to keep their vision and goals fresh and relevant to their rate of growth. If they want just a taste of Lightyear, they can begin with "Power My Future," a membership, or any other introductory Lightyear workshop.

Level Two is called "Strategic Instinct." It also contains nine principles, in addition to many new concepts dealing with how to increase innovation and imagination. Lightyear coaches can certify in this content as a next step after Level One. Using "Strategic Instinct," we bring our vision to life by integrating our right- and left-brain attributes of intuition and analysis. Level Two is designed to empower people to help families, teams, and organizations. In Chapter 16, I talk about the skills needed to recognize, raise, and resolve issues by bringing to language early senses, feelings, and vibes about what is happening. The foundational course of Level Two is "Integrated Leadership" and teaches what we call the "Five Cycles of Success," along with other Lightyear favorites such as the "Bold Request." Graduates of "Integrated Leadership" learn how to use the "Cycles of Success" to navigate leading their own projects, as well as larger team and organizational projects, by mitigating the downward spiral of miscommunication, failure to learn from failure, frustration, and disappointment.

Level Three, "Global Perspectives and Possibility," covers six Lightyear principles that deal with *going big* and expanding beyond yourself to create a global reach. It deals with the primary transformation of major structures and institutions in the fields of finance, energy, health, and human relationships. This level is the home of the principle "Get There Now," which you now understand. The foundational course of Level Three is "Whole Prosperity," which examines our definitions of wealth and helps us see new ways to invest our time and money as we assist global transformation.

If you are curious, Levels Four and Five are in the refinement stage and deal with making what Dorothy would call Universal Laws such as the Law of Harmony or the Law of Light into practical and applicable tools for living. They deal with cultures of transformation and energetic renewal and rebirth. The pathway to Lightyear mastery is established, ready and waiting for you.

You might be wondering why I didn't write my first book about the material in my first level. I had the same question. The reality is that by listening to my inner hearing and knowing, it became clear that the world is ready to "Get There Now" and make the decisions and choices that will lead to the changes and differences we are willing to make. Positive structural changes to healthcare, prisons, transportation infrastructure, corporate and country governance, air and water quality, education, and more are made by *individuals* first, and then the whole system begins its transformation. So perhaps we "Get There Now" using our Strategic Instincts to discover our Personal Power and Wholeness, or some other combination; it's all about arranging the components in different ways.

Let's return to the beginning of my journey, that dark morning at the Wellspring Spa, when I used all of the essential steps I've learned throughout my life to find my way home. Each human being has these steps available to them, yet not always in this order.

1. Return to childhood memories.

2. Listen up.

3. Journey inward and outward.

4. Ask for help. Look for Melbas.

5. Get correct information and find wonderful teachers.

6. Use the clearing switch and "take two."

7. Enter the codes of Love, Forgiveness, and Choice.

8. Get the key and "Get There Now."

Write me and let me know what you find on *your* journey. See you on Lightyear.co!

Author's Note

One of the most delightful and continuously impactful experiences of my life was traveling to Ethiopia in October 2010 with my family and a group of fabulous fundraisers. Under the unified leadership of Sapna Dayal as the Executive Director of imagine1day, Shannon Wilson as the founder, and Majka Burhardt as a professional climber and guide, we co-led an adventure trip we called "Imagine Ethiopia," raising over $100,000 to sponsor the building of a very innovative school. Imagine1day is no ordinary charity. It works with possibility and business mindsets to create schools *with* the investment and alignment of the communities they serve. Towards the end of the trip, after climbing mountains to visit continuously operational stone-carved churches, with priests who transcribe as needed the Book of Mary—yes, you heard it, the Book of Mary—onto goatskin Bibles, we gathered at the Gheralta Lodge to have a meeting with the partners of imagine1day and share some of our leadership work.

Seid Aman, the country director, a brilliant, kind young man hailing from the south of Ethiopia, offered to translate for the fifty-six people he had gathered. When I had met him ten days earlier at the Addis Ababa airport, I'd asked for his help, as my watchband was broken and I had no idea where to buy a new one on my first trip to Africa. He said, "Suzy. You are a leader. Leaders need to know what time it is. The time is now." And off he went, returning with a new band almost as quickly as I asked.

So there I was, up at the chalkboard, sharing the transformational communication work of the importance of listening as the source of true power and how to shift from fear and doubt. What happened next was nothing short of a miracle.

Seid did not translate.

Seid generated. What do I mean by generated, you ask?

Seid stood before his people and, in his language and gestures, shared about shifting the internal conversation to one of possibility, power, and choice. As he spoke, I felt with my own body sensations that Seid was radiating a radical and vital truth. Team members and partners came forward and declared new futures and their commitments to live them.

Seid and his team, over the subsequent decade, have directly led over 15,000 people in Lightyear Leadership programs, building the largest and most flourishing implementation of Lightyear Leadership in the world today, and they did all this despite great economic constraint and constant civil unrest. I am forever grateful to Seid for his generous generation of the Lightyear principles and concepts and for, as my student, showing *me* what is possible.

May you, dear reader, continue to imagine and create a wonderful world for all, now.

Acknowledgments

The writing and publication of *Get There Now* has been made possible due to the love and contribution of many, many human beings and the culmination of many, many moments. As we say in Lightyear, "Transformation is ninety-five percent logistics, and logistics is a love language."

First and foremost, gratitude to my dad, Ken Gablin, for teaching me to be bold, to belly laugh, and for granting me the "gift of the gab." To my mom, Trula Gablin, for being a Romper Room teacher, demonstrating creativity and intuition to this day, and for the gift of knowing how to send loving energy through a camera.

To my sister, Dory, for her love of language and her eternal protection.

To my husband, Brett, for always believing that I am a gift, for letting me squeeze his hand within an inch of his life while important things happen, and for always standing in the back row of my programs, doing some type of exercise, and smiling wide with his glorious front-tooth gap (recognizable even with my fuzzy right eye).

To my eldest son, Surya, for raising ourselves together amidst the chaos of me learning how to parent, for being a great husband to Mandy and dad to Rhyder and Scout, and for bringing old soul energy into our family with such love and stability. To Chandra for teaching me about unconditional love, passion, how the brain works, *and* for causing me to meet my teacher Dorothy Wood Espiau. Who knew?! To Hunter, my only daughter, for being brave enough to release negative inherited legacies from me while in my presence and for living the life of a true artist. For holding me in the firm and gentle inquiry of accountability—"Are you writing, Mom?" To Curtiss, for taking me to one hundred reptile shows, fishing boats, and aquariums to teach me to love all of God's creepy-crawler squirmy and slimy beings as my own. For diving the deep and teaching me deep faith.

To Melissa Lane, for her steadfast love of language and its precision and her capacity to bring structure to ideas. She told me early in the creation of Lightyear content the importance of books and is a confirmed bibliophile. To Matt Hoglund, for standing by me as a tall tree of wisdom. He saw I could become an author before I did. To Sophie Allen, for her gentleness, awareness, and strength as we launched lightyear.co. To Sapna Dayal, for her vision of imagine-1day and her capacity to see pathways for transformation where none existed before. To Dianne Dickerson, for taking me to Mt. Rainier to get started on *Get There Now*, and for warming me up in her cabin after I finally got back into mine.

To Chip and Shannon Wilson, for trusting me with the people of their wonderful company and non-profit. To the fabulous and beautiful people of lululemon, who set their problems down and together lit them on fire and built a transformative light for all the world to see! To human pioneers such as Parker Pearson-Maurer, for being the first lululemon leader to learn the Gems of Excellence, and to Paige Kerr, for helping start lululemon USA with us. To Deanne and Delaney Schweitzer, for being innate transformational leaders and community builders, and love to Daria Matza for being our first videographer. To Chloe Gow-Jarrett, Margo Wheeler, and her team, for co-creating at least a thousand hours of Lightyear Intensives known as Drishtis, Leadership Conferences, and Ambassador Summits. For this category of contribution, I am at a loss for words. I was granted an extended moment in time to positively alter the lives of lululemon executives, staff, ambassadors, and guests for almost a decade and a half. The loving power of lululemon diaspora and their children will be guiding this planet for generations to come.

To Steve Rio, for seeing a digital future while I was still learning how to use Gmail. To Michael Abraham, for creating our first lightyear.co user interface. To JJ Wilson, my nephew, for believing in the power of mentorship from the younger generation, and for teaching me to receive its vision.

To Igsaan Salie, our digital PM, and the world-class team at Jungle Devs who helped build our ship called lightyear.co so this book can rest on her solid decks. Thank you, Slack, Google, Zoom. Thank you, Steve Jobs, Bill and Melinda Gates, for your heart, your ease, and your love of the future.

To Seid Aman, my partner in Ethiopia, who for over ten years has cultivated the possibility of guiding an entire nation of 110 million people into the reality of their vision and goals. Seid's team has directly led over 15,000 people in Ethiopia through Lightyear, touching 500,000 more.

To Jacob Bain, for traveling to Africa with us and creating the great short film *Shareback Your Leadership*, and for his visual and musical artistry in creating our content videos, which many of you will see as your next step after reading *Get There Now*.

To Mo Jessa of Earls Kitchen + Bar, for his giant heart, and to Laura Appleton, for being the mayor of Arc'teryx and sharing her hilarious stories with British style.

To everyone that ever studied and believed in igolu, I thank you for understanding that to reach the world on time and in time, we needed to no longer be igolu. Thank you for your love and patience and kindness. Thank you for letting go of the river's edge. You give me room to breathe, know, and belong.

To the many leaders of Lightyear, our faculty, Nancy Sheridan Perry of Houston, Texas, Jacki Carr of Evergreen, Colorado, and Rebecca Bligh of Vancouver, British Columbia; to the Senior Lightyear coaches, Daniel McCall, Nicole Tsong, Erin Anderson, Jess Munion, Alex Pulfer, and Andrew Barclay; to the inaugural LCT2020 Cohort— dear God—have you ever been fun and amazing; let's all go the distance and deliver new choice-based futures to the world!

To my friend Dr. Velinda Paranal, MD, for doing every class, course, trip to Africa, Central America, zoom-God-knows-what, and every Dorothy gathering; for flying, driving, swimming, and hiking to anything I proposed, and for being so intelligent, committed, and *fun*!

To Amanda Casgar, for getting the *Livin' It Up* booklets printed in 2009 to help us raise the first $100K for imagine1day, for being insistent for twelve years that I write a book on choice, and for introducing me to Greenleaf Publishing.

To Erin Brown, my developmental editor, for her clarity, humor, her hats on our Zoom calls, and for being a "Melba." For the integrated team at Greenleaf for their logistical structure: such a love language!

To the powerful and playful Lightyear Ops team and Lightyear Champions—you wholeheartedly demonstrate that your "Giving Is Your Living." Thank you for supporting the growth of Lightyear during COVID-19 while I was off writing a book!

Finally, to Dorothy Wood Espiau, for making me draw with colored pencils when she saw that I was too "neck up" and for helping me learn how to lead her work while she was still on the planet. Thank you, Dr. Kam Kettering, for stepping up and in as her successor. I am grateful to all the beings of this Earth and beyond that gather to support humans on this great journey of rapid and radical transformation. May we become the gift and the giver, the blessed and the blessing for all time, all realities, all dimensions. TGBTGFA.

Thank you, dear reader, for listening,
With love,
Susanne

About the Author

Susanne Conrad is the founder of Lightyear Leadership, and is one of the few global women leaders and entrepreneurs in the personal development and leadership space. She was the co-developer of lululemon's renowned leadership culture and served as Director of Possibility at lululemon from 2007-2017. Susanne has over 30 years of experience transforming tens of thousands of lives across the globe and revolutionizing culture at hundreds of organizations, including TOMS, Kit and Ace, Earls Kitchen + Bar, and imagine1day.

Susanne trains, develops, and certifies leaders around the world. The Lightyear Leadership programs she leads alongside educational leadership programs in Mozambique and Ethiopia create a unified force for positive transformation among students, teachers, government ministers, and community leaders.

Susanne is a storyteller who will restore your peculiarity and empower you to be who you came to be. She demonstrates powerful inner listening and has a deep connection to a higher power. Susanne sees the best in all people and their full potential, no matter their background or walk of life. She has the ability to challenge and gently coach people through hard things and is an agenda-free champion for people's goals, vision, and success.

Susanne hails from Vashon island in the Pacific Northwest. When not leading progressive programs at Lightyear, she is leading dance and movement, adventuring in her Sprinter Van named Gloria, and laughing with her friends and family.

Made in the USA
Coppell, TX
20 January 2022